GW01605281

Depression and Anxiety Relief for Adults

The Beneficial Effects of Cognitive Behavioral Therapy on Anxiety and Depression and Ways to Use it to Your Advantage

Rhonda Jenkins

Contents

7 SIMPLE AND EFFECTIVE WAYS

TO BATTLE ANXIETY AND DEPRESSION WITHOUT MEDICATION

The Effective Strategies You Can Use on Your Own to Cope with Anxiety and Depression

Email RhondaJenkins786@gmail.com for your free copy

Rhonda Jenkins

Email: RhondaJenkins786@gmail.com
for your free copy of
The 7 Ways To Battle Anxiety

"The only impossible journey is the one you never begin."
~ Tony Robbins

Chapter 1:

Introduction

Each year, approximately one in four Americans will suffer from some type of anxiety disorder. This is the most common form of mental illness diagnosed in the United States.

Having experienced severe personal trauma, I know firsthand exactly how debilitating and crippling each of these anxiety disorders can be. I say this because chances are that, like me, this anxiety will be accompanied by stress and depression. As hard as it is to admit publicly, there were many times when these were accompanied by suicidal thoughts. All that I can say is that I'm grateful to still be here and to be able to share some of the things that changed my life for the better. It was so challenging to explain to well-intentioned friends and family members exactly what I was going through.

The truth is that unless someone has been in your situation, they have no idea of the depths of despair you feel. When your whole world seems to be turned upside down and all you can do is feel completely helpless and hopeless. The only thoughts you have are shrouded in negativity. Concentrating on anything for longer than a few minutes is futile because your thoughts are hijacked and catapulted back to those filled with doubt and despair.

If these were the only symptoms of stress, anxiety, depression, and other mental health disorders I was trying to deal with, it may have been manageable. The problem was that there was just so much more to each of them. It was like being on an emotional roller coaster without having the luxury of the ride ending... One moment, everything seemed fine, as though the dark clouds were beginning to disperse and shafts of light seemed to be fighting their way through; the next, I was filled with fear and trepidation. Thoughts of sadness, guilt, remorse, and just pure gut-wrenching mental anguish would take hold.

It was only once I realized that there was no way I could do it on my own any longer that I discovered cognitive-behavioral therapy (CBT). I needed to find a better way of trying to cope with my thoughts, emotions, and subsequent behavior. Leaving it would have surely led to self-destruction. My initial introduction to CBT was a one-on-one session and chatting with a therapist telephonically. This progressed to attending group counseling sessions regularly.

While there are plenty of resources when it comes to self-help online, most of these include a large component of positive thinking. The main difference between this and CBT is that instead of trying to simply think your way to happiness, CBT targets the problem you are experiencing now. It works on your emotions as they are now, in the moment, and through realistic thought. Don't get me wrong, I'm not knocking the power of positive thinking. It may work well for someone who has the odd day feeling down. There's a big difference between suffering from long-term mental ailments and having occasional bad days. No amount of positive thinking is a solution to anxiety, stress, depression, or any other serious mental health-related illness.

There were many things that led to my own, personal journey with mental illness, and I'm going to list them here because I need you to know that I get it. I understand exactly what you're going through because I've been there. There were many days when I felt immense sadness, depression, and just down. This often led to me simply not wanting to do anything but lying in bed all day, with the covers pulled over my head. I wasn't in the mood to see anyone, not even my nearest and dearest friends and family. My thoughts would default to those of impending doom. I kept feeling as though something was about to go wrong and there was nothing, I could do about it. This terrified me for no apparent reason, yet to me, it was all real.

Earlier, I spoke about the roller coaster of emotions. Well, that was me. One moment I would feel almost euphoric, and the next in the darkest pit ever. There never seemed to be a middle ground – that place where I could say I felt normal. This was my reality. If you're reading this book right now, chances are you can identify where I'm coming from.

I'd turn down invitations to social events or family functions because leaving the safety and security of my own home was painful. Panic attacks would follow where my chest would tighten, my heart would pound, my palms would sweat, and I felt immobilized. Even running basic errands like buying groceries was left until the very last moment when I would have to force myself. All the while, praying for it to be over. I'd go when I knew the stores would be quiet and I didn't need to face too many people.

When it came to mood swings, I would fly into fits of rage regularly for no apparent reason. Even the smallest of things, that others would dismiss as being insignificant, would get to me. This meant hurting those I love with scathing words that we all know can never be taken back. They didn't understand that I wasn't in control of my moods.

Of course, there were many other signs and symptoms that I experienced, but for the sake of brevity I'm going to list these below:

- Experiencing aches and pains that are unexplained.
- Feelings of helplessness and hopelessness took hold.
- I constantly felt anxious and worried.
- I felt sad, and my moods were low constantly.
- I felt tearful all the time.
- I had no energy whatsoever.
- I avoided visiting or socializing with friends.
- I was irritable and intolerant of those around me.
- I was no longer interested in participating in anything and lost interest in hobbies that I had once enjoyed.
- I often think about committing suicide.
- It was difficult to make decisions, even simple ones.
- My self-esteem was almost non-existent.

You may experience some of these symptoms:

- Finding it difficult to concentrate, being confused about what's going on. Connecting the dots. Close to suffering from Attention Deficit Hyperactivity Disorder (ADHD). This is a disorder that affects your ability to concentrate for long periods. In most cases, this results in restlessness. This would account for the "hyperactivity" side of this condition.
- Feeling tired most of the time, although being able to sleep is elusive (insomnia) because too many thoughts occupy your mind.
- Feeling detached from reality, including delusions, paranoia, or hallucinations.
- Helplessness in coping with daily problems or stress.

- Trouble understanding and relating to situations and people.
- Having problems with alcohol. While this never got to the point where this was a full-blown addiction, I used it as a crutch. The reason for me doing this was to try and forget what was going on in my life, even if this was just for a while.
- Major changes in eating habits could lead to weight gain or loss (something else to worry about).
- Changes in your sex drive
- Excessive anger, hostility, or violence.

Some of the things I had to deal with personally were:

- Fear
- Working long hours and excessively
- Lack of sleep, or disturbed sleep
- Trouble with relationships
- Moving back home
- Changing my child's school
- Negative attitudes

Maybe you've had to face hardships or traumatic events in your life that have been the catalyst for unstable mental health and patterns of negative thinking and behavior. Some examples of struggles include:

- The Covid pandemic
- Deaths of loved ones
- Relationship problems
- Financial challenges
- Divorce, or separation
- Emotional manipulation by others
- Loss of work
- Toxic, harmful, and painful relationships with others
- Unexpected changes and failures in your personal, professional, and social lives

Maybe you have lost your confidence and trust in the possibility of a happy life.

You often don't feel good because of negative thoughts and emotions and don't know where to get support. Advice from family and friends can offer helpful advice, but it's not always long-lasting. I found their advice and support helpful.

Maybe you've heard of CBT but cannot afford CBT or counseling sessions with a psychologist. Let's face it, CBT consultations and appointments with a therapist are often inconvenient and difficult to fit into your schedule. They are also time-consuming. You may have children with no one to look after them while you see a therapist. At least, this is what I experienced. Maybe you have tried some self-care and mental health techniques before which have not worked, or have worked temporarily, but negative thoughts and emotions always return. Without realizing it, you have become addicted to negative thought patterns. You think about harming yourself, and don't see an escape from where you are now. By the end of this book, you will be able to apply several of these strategies on your own and at your own time.

We are all likely to go through times in our lives where our emotions become overwhelmed. This doesn't fall into the categories that I am talking about. Mainly because these experiences last for a short while, and then you can return to a normal life.

In my own life, anxiety, and depression often paralyzed me. I withdrew from the world, not wanting or accepting help from anyone. I felt that there was no solution to the black hole that I felt trapped inside. Anxiety led to panic attacks. I would only leave home when I had to. Call it anti-social, I simply can't do crowds or people for that matter. Everything made me feel anxious and nervous. I battled to sleep, eat, and even think about things rationally. My concentration was impaired, my chest tightened making it hard to breathe, and my thoughts were permanently negative. I simply couldn't think of any solution(s) to what I was facing.

You may be wondering what this book is going to do for you? How is it going to get you through what you are currently experiencing when you have already tried several things that just haven't worked? To answer this question, Depression and Anxiety Relief for Adults: The Beneficial Effects of Cognitive Behavioral Therapy on Anxiety and Depression and Ways to Use it to Your Advantage has been written especially with you in mind.

Even if you've never heard of CBT, you will be able to use this book and the techniques in it. You don't need to rely on the help of a medical practitioner because CBT can be easily self-directed. CBT practitioners themselves guide their patients to self-monitor and work on themselves outside of therapy sessions. CBT isn't an average self-care guide that tells you to meditate, think happy thoughts, and let go. This is a clinical, active approach to changing your thoughts, emotions, and behaviors. Mental health researchers have discovered that self-directed CBT can be just as effective as working with a therapist.

You will gain insight into:

- What Cognitive Behavioral Therapy (CBT) is.
- How you can apply these techniques at home yourself.
- How to use CBT methods to maintain healthy mental wellbeing anytime.
- There are practical exercises, worksheets, and CBT methods included that will help you to:
- Have basic self-help for early interventions.
- It will provide you with CBT strategies that will change thought patterns, override negative emotions, and help you engage in healthy behavior.
- Become aware of mental health, depression, and anxiety.
- How to maintain your mental health during future tough times, toxic relationships, hardships, and life's challenges.

You will be able to determine the best way for you to live a happy, healthy, and meaningful life using the techniques provided in this book. You can get rid of any type of irrational thoughts and beliefs that have been deeply rooted within the subconscious due to any incidents, patterns, and past experiences. You will understand what CBT is and how it can assist you in your life – without any difficult terms. It is suitable, even if you have no prior knowledge of CBT. You will be able to maintain a healthy mindset and behavior no matter what and know exactly what to do in the future, how to deal with negativity and difficult situations.

Apart from the reasons I've already mentioned, I had to go through many failed attempts before I found something that was going to work to treat all my symptoms. Some of these included stress management techniques, attending antidepressants, and anti-anxiety classes. Each of these provided me with ways to live a better and healthier life. I've been using CBT methods and stress management exercises and have seen firsthand how my life has changed for the better. This has had a positive effect on my mental well-being.

Since then, I have been anxiously engaged in learning more by attending many classes led by professionals in this field. I only use therapeutically proven techniques because mental health is so important.

This book gives simple and practical Cognitive Behavioral Therapy (CBT) techniques you can use at home to guide yourself through dark times in your life to take care of your mental health. You will learn the CBT methods to use for battling stress, anxiety, and depression.

When asked why writing this book is so important to me, it's quite simple really... From personal experience, I have learned that I need to value myself first and foremost. Another reason for writing this book is to help those who are suffering from depression and anxiety for whatever reason. I would like to encourage you to look after your mental health. Whatever is done, is done. There are many reasons to live a life filled with happiness. Life is a blessing from God. You first need to love yourself, no matter what bad things happen in your life.

I understand what it's like to suffer from a mental illness. I get that not everyone has the time or money to spend seeking professional help from psychiatrists. Because of this, they continue to suffer without having the means or tools necessary to deal with these things. I'm writing this book because I have personally seen how powerful CBT can be, and there are so many ways you can use these techniques yourself.

Before we dive right in, I want you to know that there is always light and hope at the end of the tunnel, no matter what challenges you're facing.

Chapter 2:

Cognitive Behavioral Therapy: The Holistic Approach

"Positive psychology is not remotely intended to replace therapy or pharmacology. So, when depressed, anxious or in panic or post-traumatic stress disorder, I am all for therapies that will work. Positive psychology is another arrow in the quiver of public policy and psychology through which we can raise wellbeing above zero."

~ Martin Seligman

On the 25th of November 2017, I was waiting for my husband to return from work. Usually, he would always be home by 8 p.m. It was now 10 p.m. with no word, or sign from him. His phone was switched off. Nonetheless, I tried calling him about 100 times. Besides myself with worry, I never had his work number and began to expect the worst.

At first, I thought he was with friends, and simply lost track of time. Slowly, my mind is filled with all sorts of negative things. I was 32 weeks pregnant with our second child. A complicated pregnancy didn't make things easier at all. I was stressed constantly because there was no news of his whereabouts. The night was spent tossing and turning. Tears flowed relentlessly. Negative thoughts were swimming in my head. Trying to explain how bad that evening was, seems impossible right now.

He finally returned home at 8 a.m. the following morning, sobbing constantly. He remained silent about what had happened no matter how many times I asked him what had happened, or what was wrong. He finally opened up only to tell me that he had been arrested and was out on bail.

Then, the investigations started as they were trying to build a case against him. I was living in constant fear that he was going to be arrested again. This naturally led to stress, depression, and concern for my unborn child. Each time I had stomach cramps I was convinced I was in early labor. I couldn't stop thinking that something bad was going to happen.

To cut a long story short, the following two years were filled with way more downs than ups. Mental health problems began shortly after the birth of my child. Trying to imagine what I was going through is difficult for most people to wrap their heads around.

It took two years of investigations and upheavals before the trial finally started. After two solid weeks in court, he was convicted and imprisoned for 14 years. This was the worst day of my life. I felt broken and shattered. Thoughts of killing myself seemed rational at the time. After what I believed to have been 10 years of a happy marriage, everything was crumbling right before my eyes. I had lost my husband and didn't know how I was going to live without him. What about my children? How were they going to live without their daddy?

The subsequent days and nights were just so painful. The children cried for their daddy all the time. I had no idea of what to tell them or do to make them feel better. Not knowing where to go for help, I felt completely hopeless.

Because it was such a high-profile case, it was featured in major news outlets and covered by the media. It wasn't long before all my friends and family would find out the truth. I was ashamed. The public began attacking our home and targeted his family. I kept indoors for a long time. My older son couldn't attend school. The community turned on us, making life unbearable. When things reached a boiling point, I finally had to file a police report. Social workers became involved and advised us to leave our home and move from the area.

From this time, I began to struggle as a single mother with two children. Homeless, for the next couple of months I will move between different relatives' homes, sleeping on the sofa or the floor. During this time, both of my children had bad chickenpox. Watching them suffer killed me inside. I couldn't stand the fact that they were suffering so much and couldn't even sleep in a proper bed because I was homeless.

The social housing system was a long process, but they were finally able to provide us with accommodation. This was far away from my family and friends, my support structure at the time. This forced me to look for private accommodation, which was extremely challenging because I had no job, no money, and no savings.

Severe depression and anxiety set in. Therefore, I had to ask for professional help. This led me to CBT. With the help of CBT and support from others, I was able to finally come out of a very dark situation. I am now living happily with my two children.

Whenever I remember this period of my life, I still feel like that shattered and broken woman. Everything is a nightmare, even now. As I'm writing this, memories come flooding back and I can't stop the tears from flowing.

Let me explain how this relates to cognitive behavioral therapy—there was a series of incidents that occurred (the disappearance of my husband, and his arrest and conviction).

This led to negative thinking (things like "how am I going to face anyone, I feel so ashamed, what am I going to tell my children?" "how are we meant to survive?") many other thoughts were racing through my mind at the time, but I think you get the picture.

Of course, this thinking led to all sorts of emotions—fear, dread, impending doom, anxiety, stress, and severe depression.

My behavior? I functioned in preservation mode. Even though I was trying to do the very best I could for my children and my family, nothing seemed enough. I felt like a failure—as a friend, daughter, and most of all, as a mother. Not knowing what was going to happen from one day to the next was driving me insane. This is when severe depression set in and took over my life.

It's important to understand that when you go through a psychological experience, the way you interpret situations becomes distorted. This in turn harms the actions you decide to take when faced with the same situation in the future.

This chapter will explain exactly what CBT is. The core principles of CBT theory and practice consist of changing thinking, leading to changing emotions, and using techniques to change behavior. The focus will be on the benefits of CBT and why it can be used as a self-help method. Finally, it will prepare you to start your very own journey using some of the simple CBT techniques I will share with you in the chapters that follow.

CBT in Simple Terms

Simplified, CBT is built around the principle of cognition (which is the way we think), entwined with emotions (the way we feel), which influences how we behave, and what actions we do or don't take.

This can be clearly seen in the illustration of a basic cycle:

Cognitive Behavioral Therapy Basic Cycle

There is a direct relationship between our thoughts, our emotions or feelings, and our behavior. What we think at any given moment leads to negative, destructive emotions, which in turn lead us to behave irrationally.

With CBT, you can become aware of negative thinking as well as how you misinterpret these thoughts, you can then break the cycle of behavior that supports these negative thoughts. It's changing your thoughts by becoming aware of what you are thinking at any given moment, analyzing, or assessing each of these thoughts. It's challenging your thinking to determine whether they're actual reality, or whether they're a figment of your imagination. Has your thinking been influenced, or distorted because of something that has happened to you?

CBT works on things that are happening to you now. It's important to understand that some life events remain locked up in the back of our minds only to resurface unexpectedly in the present. Believe it or not, this happens often. You may be wondering whether CBT can help you deal with things that have possibly happened in your childhood. The truth is that if these memories have surfaced now and are causing you to think negatively, and act irrationally, then absolutely.

CBT—The Basics

Let's briefly discuss the different components that make up CBT. We will expand on many of these basic concepts in the chapters that follow.

Cognitive

The Merriam Webster dictionary (n.d.) defines cognition as "conscious mental activities: the activities of thinking, understanding, learning, and remembering." This means that when we're thinking negatively, chances are we will begin to believe these thoughts about ourselves.

Negative thoughts about ourselves start here.

Beck's Theory of Cognitive Distortions

In 1967, one of the forefathers and founders of what was then only referred to as Cognitive Theory (CT), Aaron Beck, proposed another cycle relating to cognition. He theorized that if we saw the world in a negative light, this in turn would lead to only seeing a future filled with negativity. These two distorted beliefs would then lead to thinking and believing negative things about ourselves. These concepts would become known as "Beck's cognitive triad."

Essentially, the triad, or triangle, consists of three main components relating to how we see things:

- How we see ourselves
- How we see the world
- How we see the future

Some examples of this might include:

- Ourselves – "I'm so dumb" or "I'm a total failure."
- The world – "Nobody even notices me."
- The future – "What's the point, the world is doomed anyway."

Behavior

One of the main aims of CBT is to help you try and change patterns of behavior that are harmful, or negative. This is done by challenging and facing up to the things we fear the most. Much of the emphasis is placed on changing the way we think. You may not even realize that you're negatively thinking most of the time. It's done on autopilot. Only once you can identify each of these negative thoughts will you be able to work through a process of being able to see how they're influencing the way you behave.

CBT Self-help Strategies

Let me first say that when it comes to CBT, there are so many different psychological conditions that it can be seen as an overarching treatment, or solution to anything from anxiety, stress, and depression to treating obsessive-compulsive disorder (OCD), finding ways to cope in the workplace. These are just a handful of a long list of issues. It can even help with physical pain, which is quite believable when you think about it. Many of the emotions we feel when we're experiencing negativity at its worst are physically painful.

It's easy to understand that if CBT is so effective in treating so many different health conditions that there are almost as many different strategies that can be used to treat them. Some of these techniques could include:

- Goal setting - Strategies to work on goals that are meaningful and relevant to what you are currently going through.
- Identifying negative thoughts - Tools to help you analyze your thoughts. Being realistic and working in the present.
- Journaling - Learning to write things down can help you gain perspective on where your thoughts, emotions, or behavior is coming from. These techniques can also help you pinpoint where your emotions are coming from.
- Mental distractions - Tools to help you direct your focus away from negative emotions. How to replace negative thinking.
- Practicing new skills - Ways to identify new hobbies and interests. Learning new things to keep your mind from leaning toward destructive thinking.
- Problem-solving - How to look for ways to solve problems that happen because of negative thinking.
- Relaxation techniques - Ways to relax your muscles, to relieve stress and tension. Guided meditation, yoga, exercise, and various other solutions.
- Roleplay - Normally used to deal with phobias, by working through various scenarios, eventually building up to the point where you can face your fears.

- Self-monitoring - Teaching how to be more aware of behavior patterns and how these influence your surroundings. Finding ways to change behavior for positive outcomes.

Why CBT Works

One of the main reasons why CBT is so successful is that it focuses on educating you that while you may not be able to control the natural flow of the world, you certainly have control over the way you interpret your environment. This leads to you having the power to make rational, realistic decisions when it comes to your behavior.

You can change the way you think about certain things. Much of our thinking is habitual. The longer you allow yourself to feed your negative thoughts and beliefs, the longer you'll remain in the same destructive cycle. It requires awareness of each thought. Being able to assess them to test whether they are realistic, and relevant to your life right now. Is your negative thinking doing anything to serve you right now? If not, it's time to get rid of them. If you do this, you can break the vicious cycle that holds so many of us captive in a never-ending loop of negativity. You're able to change your moods.

Another reason why CBT is so effective is that it doesn't take forever to see results. It's best to work on one issue at a time. Focused CBT can be done by yourself. You don't always need to find and pay for a therapist. Don't get me wrong, I am not knocking psychologists or therapists. My point is that you can still use CBT techniques at home, or anywhere you are at any time of the day without having to save up to see a therapist. This could save you both time, and money. According to the National Alliance on Mental Illness (NAMI) CBT can be an effective form of treatment even when self-directed (Nami, n.d.).

What Can CBT Help With?

- Alcohol addiction or abuse
- Anger management

- Anorexia (eating disorder)
- Anxiety
- Bipolar
- Borderline personality disorder
- Bulimia (eating disorder)
- Chronic fatigue syndrome (CFS)
- Chronic health anxiety disorder
- Death of a loved one
- Depression
- Drug dependency
- Fibromyalgia
- Hoarding
- Insomnia
- Irritable bowel syndrome (IBS)
- Obsessive-compulsive disorder (OCD)
- Panic attacks
- Panic disorder
- Perinatal problems affecting mental health
- Phobias
- Post-traumatic stress disorder (PTSD)
- Psychosis
- Schizophrenia
- Self-harm
- Sexual abuse - including rape, incest, and molestation

As you can see, there are so many conditions that CBT strategies can help you with, so why not try it out and see for yourself how it can change your life for good? Even though I had no idea what CBT was when I first started, I decided to give it a go. CBT got me through some of the darkest moments of my life. If you want to see real change, if you're trying to deal with any of the above conditions, give CBT a chance to help you too. Change takes place a lot quicker and is healthier than pumping yourself full of prescription drugs.

What CBT is not

As with many treatments, there are misinterpretations of what CBT is as a form of therapy. We'll briefly touch on what some of these misconceptions are.

Many people are under the impression that cognitive behavioral therapy is simply observes your thoughts to manage your thought process. As I've explained above, there are three components that make up successful CBT. Action needs to be taken to change the way you think to ultimately changing unhealthy behavior.

No matter how positive you think you are, how many self-help books you read or listen to that appeal to any form of positive thinking isn't the only part of CBT. Sure, positive thinking does form part of it, but it's not the be-all and end-all of this therapy. CBT will teach you how to think realistically about your current situation, and even past events to deal with them.

It's also not just about shifting your thoughts from negative to positive. Many people have the misconception that because CBT deals with the here and now, there's no hope for those having difficulty coming to terms with things that may have happened to them in their childhood. CBT is a very effective form of treatment when it comes to dealing with past experiences, no matter how long ago they took place. Any issues or emotions linked to these experiences may only manifest themselves when you are much older. A minor can act as a trigger, unlocking these memories which can be devastating.

There's only one strategy when it comes to using CBT to treat the entire spectrum of disorders or chronic conditions. The truth is that each approach and strategy differ. It is dependent on the individual and what their specific needs are.

Preparing Yourself for CBT at Home

There are a couple of things you need to know before trying to make CBT work for you from home. This will set you up for success. There are many self-help materials available online that can assist you on this journey. However, before you can expect to change, you need to be willing to change. This isn't always easy, especially when we are set in our ways. While it's not always easy, it's also not impossible. Change is not going to happen immediately or overnight. Instead, this is going to be gradual. The approach that CBT takes is extremely structured and it's important to follow each step through to the end. This is how you will gain the most from this therapy.

Chapter 3:

The Role of Negative Emotions in CBT

"One popular theory in psychology is that human beings are not evolved to be happy, but instead are 'designed' for survival" (Psychology Tools, n.d.).

Our ancestors and forefathers owed much of their survival to their emotional responses to situations. Because they lived under primitive conditions, they had to rely on these emotions to keep them safe. Emotions that we would describe as stress, anxiety, and panic today were exactly what kept them out of harm's way. As an example: If they were out hunting and heard twigs or branches snapping near them. They would immediately become more alert, their pupils would dilate, for them to see better. Hearing would become acute.

In a split decision, they would need to decide what they were going to do. They could either run away from the threat, stand up to the threat and fight in the hope that they would come out on the winning side... or, they could decide to remain completely still, waiting for the threat to pass by. For our ancestors, threats may include wild animals, inclement weather conditions, and even other people in the form of enemies, different clans, tribes, or invading marauders.

Today, we can experience these same emotions at any time. Sure, we won't necessarily have to fight off a bear or be chased by a lion, but other threats are and can be very real. Each time we feel threatened by something or someone, there are chemical changes taking place in the body.

A modern example of this could be: You may be driving on the freeway when there's a collision between a couple of cars in front of you. Your immediate reaction would be to avoid colliding with yourself. You could decide to brake, swerve out of the way, or pull to the side of the road. Because everything happens so suddenly, you don't wait to weigh up all your options. This is a life-threatening situation after all. Your brain and body will work in tandem, taking what appears to be the best possible option for self-preservation. It all happens in a split second.

Once you are safely out of harm's way, you may notice that your heart is racing, and your palms are sweating. Hearing and vision are on high alert. Depending on each situation, there will be emotions that you experience. These are negative emotions, but we need them, so we know when we're in danger. It's only once you are free and clear that you can look back and see that your thinking may have been slightly distorted, or unreasonable at the time. In the above example, you might become angry, shouting loud obscenities to the other drivers, and even the accident victims themselves.

Please understand that these emotions, reactions, and behavior happen automatically. (In that split second). Once we can look back at our thoughts and behave rationally, we may be able to see that most of these emotional outbursts were unnecessary. Our behavior and actions may have been irrational at the time, and they helped to save our lives.

The Reason Behind Emotions

Everything we do is because of emotions. These emotions lead to how we act. They help us decide on the best course of action in any situation. In a nutshell, we won't be able to survive without having emotions to rely on. How different would your life be without being able to feel things for yourself? I'm not talking about physical touch, but rather emotions. What would it be like to try to communicate with your loved ones, or interact with your children or grandchildren? I can think of nothing worse than feeling dead inside. Unable to express yourself.

Centuries ago, man evolved to make critical, life-saving decisions for themselves. This was done by weighing the pros and cons. This 'instinct' helped make the right decisions. Emotions led them to behave according to the situation. Think about it, because of evolution, our first ancestors knew what was best for them. They knew what meats to eat to remain healthy, which berries, and plants were good for them, and those that possibly make them ill.

It's believed that we belong to the same family as animals. If you've ever been watching animals, you've probably realized that they learned to do everything by instinct. They've learned what to avoid (anything bad for them), and what is safe. Think about wild games roaming the savannahs, they're constantly alert for danger. This may come in the form of carnivorous animals ranging from lions, tigers, leopards, and for smaller prey, even a pack of hyenas can be fatal.

Watering holes posed their threat when other animals weren't aware of the danger just beneath the surface in the form of crocodiles or alligators. Unsuspecting prey could be innocently drinking water when a moment later, they're locked between the jaws of these ancient reptiles.

Instinctively, animals know what foods are safe for them to eat, that they need shelter and protection from predators, where to sleep, and when to escape danger. All of this is done using emotions. They can 'feel' when something is not right, and subsequently avoided, it or when it's quite safe. The feelings they would get would influence their behavior. They would either act or react.

Emotions help direct decisions we make every second of our lives. I use the word second because that's often how quickly we need to react to situations where we are in harm or danger. I'm sure you'll agree that trying to list each emotion will take up the rest of this book. Some examples of emotions and possible behaviors to follow could include:

- Feeling affectionate can inspire us to get close to others and take a chance on love.
- When we're feeling angry, we can lash out at others, attack them physically or verbally, or defend ourselves.
- Having compassion, being sympathetic, or showing empathy allows us to want to comfort those that are suffering, or simply be with them.
- If we're feeling confused, we may be driven to want to investigate things for ourselves. We may find making decisions extremely difficult. Indecision isn't healthy.
- Being confused may result in our need to further investigate to find out the facts for ourselves. It could also lead to becoming incapacitated with uncertainty because we can't decide.

- Feeling disgusted by something, someone, or a situation could result in withdrawal as a means of escape. You feel the need to get as far away as possible.
- You may want to run and hide when you feel humiliated or embarrassed. Fear can have the same effect.
- When we feel guilty, there's a need for us to make amends. We need to fix whatever we've done to make things right again.
- Feeling indifferent toward someone may cause us to ignore them.
- Finding joy and happiness in a situation can make us eager to want to join in and share in the excitement.
- If we feel powerless, it's easier for us to throw in the towel and give up rather than fight for ourselves.
- When we feel sad, we want to withdraw from society. We keep on thinking about the past, or things that have happened. We worry about it, which, of course, is futile.
- Feeling ashamed of ourselves makes us want to disappear. We need to keep secrets hidden away from the world and those around us.

I have personally experienced many of the negative emotions listed above. In many cases, I had no idea that my emotions would result in me withdrawing further and further away from those who loved me and were worried about me and my future. It was only much later that I could identify the effect that negative thinking had on me. I was angry at the world. Although I had not done anything wrong, I was ashamed. It felt as though I was a criminal, even though realistically I was just a victim of circumstances.

CBT helped me step back into the present moment to look at situations realistically. I could identify most negative emotions, trying to trace them back to their origin. I needed to tie my thinking back to how I was behaving.

The Approach and Avoid Function of Emotions

The approach part of emotions will help us confirm when it's safe to approach and accept something. Most of the time, things we can approach and accept are good for us. We can feel this instinctively. Good things lead to positive results. The opposite is avoiding emotions. You know that voice in your head that tells you that it's not safe. In most cases, things you need to avoid are harmful.

In all honesty, we should all be focused on those things that are good for us and will result in something positive. Think about choosing between junk food and a balanced diet. While a fast food meal may provide you short-term happiness or satisfaction, in the long-term it's not good for your health. The same comes to getting enough rest. Do you binge on your favorite series on Netflix, only going to sleep in the early hours of the morning, or can you limit yourself because you know you need enough rest to be able to function properly? Can you see how approach and avoidance can make a difference in your life right now?

The truth is that we are so conditioned by the 21st century that we've become comfortable rejecting those things that are good for us. It's easier to settle to keep the status quo, leaving things as they are. We don't even challenge these emotions. Instead, we rob ourselves of all the good that is out there. We push joy and happiness aside. Maybe it is because we don't feel we deserve to be happy. For this to change, we must find a way to somehow go after happiness instead of misery and sadness.

When we get into a negative headspace where the only things, we feel are fear, anger, confusion, guilt, shame, or self-loathing, we will do anything to avoid those around us. We prefer to wallow in self-pity rather than spend time with others. We turn down invitations to take part in normal, healthy activities. We chose not to socialize with friends or family. We should reject these negative emotions because they only lead to negative behavior.

Let's talk about panic attacks for a moment. When you have a panic attack, chances are you'll first feel scared. Next comes feeling powerless to do anything about the situation. This could immobilize you, keep you stuck. You're too afraid to make a move. You don't want to face anyone. You avoid all situations that could make you feel worse. You simply want to run away from these experiences. It's much easier to lock yourself up in the safety of your own home rather than take on the challenge of stepping into sunlight. You can't take a chance of finding something better than paralyzing fear and avoidance.

Because of fear, we may avoid accepting opportunities for growth that arise. Think about being offered an exciting new job. Instead of looking forward to positive change, we feel safer turning it down. We're happy to remain in a dead-end job that frustrates us and makes us question our abilities instead of taking a chance. It's comfortable for us. At least, we know we will have a steady income. There's no guarantee that the new job will work out. These are thoughts that fill your mind when your thoughts keep defaulting to the negative.

When our emotions become skewed, we can find ourselves in dangerous territory. Even positive emotions, when overdone, can be unhealthy for us. Think about socializing with friends all the time. It's easy to overdo it. When anything is done in excess, you run the risk of falling into addictive behavior. Whether it's overeating, drinking too much, taking drugs, or even over-the-counter medications. I'd like to point out that you may be taking prescription medication that you need. If you're sticking to the doctor's advice, these are necessary. It's the abuse of these drugs that I'm referring to. All addictions or abuse are bad for you, especially when battling mental health conditions.

In the following section, we are going to outline what some of these disorders are. Remember that each of us is different. You may experience all the symptoms, or only a few. If any of these resonate with you, then it's worthwhile taking a closer look at CBT as a treatment method to help you cope.

Anxiety

"I'm trying to stay as calm as possible and focus one day at a time, but when reality sets in, I feel everything: anxiety, excitement, nerves, pressure, and joy." ~ Shawn Johnson

Before you can work on anxiety disorders or issues, it would be useful to understand what anxiety is, where it comes from, and some of the symptoms. This will help you determine whether you are suffering from anxiety or any other anxiety-related problems.

Firstly, it's quite natural for each of us to go through normal worries and concerns over situations and circumstances that happen to us. An example of this could be being nervous to stand in front of a large group of people to deliver a speech or presentation. Once you're done, the anxiety will subside and eventually disappear altogether. This is not an anxiety-related disorder. Long-term anxiety lasts for more than a month, and it is ongoing.

Anxiety is when you worry about things constantly. You may feel like something's about to go wrong, but you don't know what. You're nervous all the time, your muscles are tense, making you feel like you're always on edge. Other physical symptoms could include:

- Not being able to sleep because your mind is racing all the time. You're focused on worrying about things you have no control over.
- Your heart is beating much faster than normal.
- Because you're worried so much you can't concentrate properly.
- You are shaking and can't control it.
- You feel tired all the time, no matter how much sleep you get.
- No matter how hard you try, you can't control worry.
- You avoid situations because everything comes across as a threat.

Anxiety can easily be triggered by too many people, situations that are overstimulating like bright lights, loud music. Even shopping malls and stores can lead to further anxiety. It's constantly having that fear in the pit of your stomach that something is wrong, yet you don't know what it is. In many cases, anxiety is triggered by something. The big thing is that it interferes with being able to function normally from day to day.

Bipolar Disorder

"Because of my bipolar disorder, I tend to have these mixed states, which are depressed but loud and agitated. Therefore, I can be terribly irritable. I go to cognitive behavioral therapy in order not to yell at my children." ~ Ayelet Waldman

This mental illness often goes untreated, and this can have a negative effect not only on the person with the illness but also on those around them. You may think that it's quite rare. On the contrary, it's more common than you would imagine. You will be able to recognize this illness through severe mood swings. One minute, you're fine, happy, and a pleasure to be around. The next minute you're in the depths of despair.

For anyone suffering from bipolar, it's not something that they've asked for and they can't control their moods. This is one of the ways to correctly diagnose this disorder. I must just mention that you could experience both moods at the same time, making it extremely confusing and even more frustrating.

If you've heard the term 'manic depressive' this is a great description of bipolar disorder. Let's look at each of these symptoms under each heading.

Manic Depressive - Highs

Key symptoms of mania are as follows:

- become distracted easily
- long periods of feeling happy (high)
- you don't need to sleep as much

- extreme impulsiveness and restlessness
- risky behavior - gambling away life savings, irresponsible shopping sprees
- speak fast because your thoughts are racing
- being overconfident in your capabilities

For symptoms of depression, refer to the 'symptoms' section below.

If you can see yourself in these symptoms and descriptions, the good news is that CBT can help you. Most people think that this disorder can only be treated by psychiatrists and prescription drugs. While many forms of bipolar can be regulated with scheduled drugs, it has been found that behavioral therapy can go a long way to ease symptoms.

Depression

"You say you're 'depressed'—all I see is resilience. You are allowed to feel messed up and inside out. It doesn't mean you're defective—it just means you're human." ~ David Mitchell, (Cloud Atlas)

Where anxiety fills your mind with worry, depression is when you're constantly down. You're no longer interested in doing things that once used to entertain or excite you. You have no interest in socializing. In short, chances are you feel that it would be easier to give up rather than go on living. Unfortunately, not everyone understands depression and often friends and family members try to tell you to "just get over it," or to "snap out of it." While they mean well, a major depressive disorder isn't something that you can simply shrug off. Much like an anxiety disorder, these symptoms need to last for an extended period for your mood to be classified or diagnosed as depression.

It's quite normal for you to feel depressed for a while when you've just had a baby, or when someone close to you dies. Each of these is a normal reaction to these circumstances and will certainly pass given some time. If these moods persist for longer than a month or so, then you may want to double-check whether you're not suffering from depression.

Common symptoms of depression that last every day for almost the whole day include:

- Feeling sad for no reason. You may cry for no reason and find it difficult to control feelings of hopelessness.
- It's easy to lose your temper over the smallest thing. Often expressing your anger and frustration vocally. It's not directed at anyone. You're irritable and no fun to be around.
- Doing anything is exhausting. You hardly have any energy and feel tired all the time.
- You've lost interest in things that you found enjoyable and exciting before. This could include anything from playing a sport, visiting friends and family, and even sex.
- There's a problem with sleeping. Either you can't sleep at all, or you sleep too much. You may even be able to sleep but wake up with nightmares or general restlessness.
- You feel the same symptoms as anxiety and feeling restless.
- Physical problems can occur. Some of these may include unexplained headaches, back pain, and tension throughout the body. These are not a result of injury or illness.
- You feel guilty and things that have happened in the past. There have possibly been circumstances in your life that have made you feel worthless.
- Eating is a problem. Either you lose your appetite and lose weight, or you turn to food as a sense of comfort. Weight gain will follow. This often leads to something else being depressed about.
- Your self-talk is only negative, and you spend most of the time beating yourself up over the least little thing.
- Decision-making is a challenge. Concentrating is tough. You can't even remember some of the simplest yet most important things. Even your reflexes are slower.
- Thoughts of death and suicide are never far away. You may have even attempted suicide before.

Instead of making the right choices about our health and well-being, we choose to withdraw. We avoid facing the facts of incidents or experiences that have happened, rather than working through each problem systematically. It's getting into such a low mood that you can't get out of it no matter how hard you try.

As a caveat: If you have suicidal thoughts now, please contact your nearest medical professional or a hotline as soon as possible.

Maybe you don't feel comfortable talking to a professional or anyone else about your personal problems. You need to think about things realistically. For me, it was my two children. I was worried about who was going to take care of them if I took my life. Even in my darkest days, there were important reasons for me to live. To fight through darkness and depression.

Obsessive-compulsive disorder (OCD)

"There isn't anybody out there who doesn't have a mental health issue, whether it's depression, anxiety, or how to cope with relationships. Having OCD is not an embarrassment anymore – for me. Just know that there is help and your life could be better if you go out and seek the help." ~ Howie Mandel

OCD is responsible for obsessing over things like the past. It often makes you behave in a certain way, without being able to control this behavior. Each of these can cause a string of negative emotions such as fear, anxiety, and stress. With OCD, your thoughts can be so realistic that you actually begin to believe them. A simple example of OCD is checking whether all your doors and windows are locked several times before leaving home. You get to your car and go back to recheck them. You've managed to convince yourself that you might have missed something.

Typically, when people talk about OCD, they automatically assume that the definition of this behavior is having everything being perfect around them. You know, the perfectly clean home where nothing is out of place—ever! In fact, this definition of OCD is completely wrong, especially when it comes to mental health. If you suffer from intrusive thoughts for longer than an hour a day, you may be suffering from OCD.

Two of the symptoms of OCD are:

- Compulsions
- Obsessions

Compulsions involve doing the same thing repeatedly as a means to work through stress, anxiety, or depression. An example of this would be visiting the local bar directly after work each day and remaining there until closing time. Drinking can only go so far when it comes to managing mental illness. The truth is that the problems are still there in the morning. Negative coping behavior can lead to addiction.

Being obsessed with certain thoughts can be upset. No matter how hard you try to ignore it, your mind keeps on going back there. It's living in fear that your thoughts can materialize in real life. You could be obsessed with things that have happened in the past. Of course, bringing these obsessions into the present is unhealthy and can affect both your mental health and well-being.

Panic attacks

"I knew I was having a panic attack. I hadn't had one in a while, though, and I'd forgotten how they made everything like that, and I was going to fall apart. How they reminded me of how trapped I was." ~ Elizabeth Scott

Understanding where panic attacks come from is not that easy. These attacks can strike at any time, without warning. Panic attacks are accompanied by extreme fear and discomfort. Individuals suffering from this disorder are usually afraid that they're going to have a panic attack, making everything much worse. You're unable to control the sudden onset of sheer terror. What makes panic attacks different is that they happen without warning, usually lasting for anywhere between 10 minutes to 30 minutes. There are instances where they've lasted more than an hour. Symptoms include the following:

- having difficulty breathing
- feeling lightheaded or dizzy (vertigo)
- The heartbeat is faster than normal
- The heartbeat is irregular due to stress and anxiety

- choking sensations
- battling to breathe
- tightness in your chest
- nausea
- uncontrolled shaking and trembling
- feeling detached from reality
- swing between chills and sweating
- fear of dying
- feeling numb in feet or hands
- fear of people and/or situations that take you away from your comfort zone

So, how do you deal with panic attacks? CBT can help you with this disorder. The aim is to minimize or remove negative thinking. This can be done by assessing your emotions and changing your thought process so you can reduce fear and anxiety.

- reduce caffeine intake, including stimulants like energy drinks
- get enough sleep
- stick to a regular schedule
- exercise regularly

More women than men are likely to suffer from panic attacks.

How CBT Factors Challenge Negative Emotions

Remember, we are each different and unique individuals with different thoughts and emotions acting as a driving force behind our behavior. Sometimes it's difficult to accept that our emotions can be as negative as they are. Instead of questioning why we need to experience such strong negative emotions, think about the lessons they teach us. We are human, after all, and emotions are part of our human experiences. Think about it this way, being nervous can teach us to be cautious. We may be prompted to end a destructive or dysfunctional relationship because we realize we no longer love the person we're with.

The downside is that many of our emotions are negative. These result in pain and anguish rather than giving us the opportunity to grow. Some negative emotions could include anxiety, uncertainty, feeling judged, paranoia, and hopelessness. These are just a handful of negative emotions. As you well know, none of these makes us feel good about ourselves.

We think that the negative emotions we feel are because of our thoughts and behavior. In other words, how we think and behave influences our emotions. It's easy for us to jump to conclusions instead of being rational about what's really going on internally. We believe each of these emotions to the point where they are making us ill. Mentally ill.

CBT and Emotion

According to the CBT Model of Emotions,

"If you want to learn to manage your mood and act more effectively in the face of challenging situations, it is crucial to develop the ability to identify and distinguish between thoughts, feelings, and behaviors. Usually, when we are overwhelmed, emotion feels like a tidal wave of discomfort, but we don't stop to clarify the components of that emotion. As a result, we have great difficulty doing anything about our mood other than waiting for it to pass all on its own." (Cognitive Behavioral Therapy Los Angeles, n.d.-b)

Most people believe that we have no control over our circumstances or experiences. We believe that our emotions are the result of things that happen to us. We get cut off in traffic and blame the driver of the other vehicle for making us angry. Because someone was abrupt with us, we insisted on stewing over it for days, weeks, and sometimes even years. In truth, you have no idea what the individual was going through at the time. They may have had a perfectly good reason for being discourteous on the day, and chances are extremely likely that it had nothing to do with you. CBT teaches us how to monitor and question what is taking place internally. Is it realistic, and in the present?

Thinking About Your Emotions

The following is the first of the exercises we'll work through together. This is one of the most common exercises used in CBT. You will find a blank worksheet that you can work through on your own. If you would like to design and use your worksheet, you can do this by taking a piece of paper or opening a blank page in a document on your computer. Divide the page into three equal sections. Draw a table marking the column on the far left, 'A,' the column in the center, 'B,' and the column on the far right, 'C.'

Column B, 'Belief,' and column C, 'Emotion,' are the same as the worksheet below.

Beneath column A, label the column 'Situation' with a subheading – 'What situations lead to your emotion?' Column B's subheading should read – 'What belief connects the situation and emotion?' Move over to column C. Here, the subheading should be, 'What emotions result from the situation?'

Example:

Situation – You overhear someone talking about you at work. How does this make you feel?

Emotion – Frustration, low self-esteem, embarrassment, and more... What is the result –You are ready to give up. (There may be several emotions that come from this, write each of these down.)

Repeat the same process whenever a situation occurs and you can pinpoint exactly what you are thinking, and the subsequent behavior that results from each of these. Divide them with a line or separate each event from the other. A blank worksheet follows.

Directions:

The main goal is to change our thinking. This, in turn, will help change the beliefs we internalize and ultimately the emotions that result.

Question your thinking.

Your thoughts may be internalized (that little voice you hear inside your head), maybe you experience thoughts through pictures. Please understand that our thoughts create our beliefs... Even when these beliefs aren't accurate. Are your thoughts negative? Maybe they're destructive and unrealistic. When this happens, our problems only get worse, instead of better.

Example: You receive a text message from a friend that automatically brings back memories from the past. These weren't the best times or experiences in your life. You do your best to forget about them. Maybe you've even managed to keep them locked away for several years already. What do these thoughts tell you? Are they the truth, or something you're telling yourself?

What do you believe?

Your beliefs can go one of two ways... Do you have a clear understanding of what the message is telling you, or is your mind taking you down a completely irrational path? Are your beliefs about the text taking you to a positive or negative place? Can you tell the difference between the two? If you're thinking negatively, question where the belief comes from. Is it valid, or something you're telling yourself?

Finally,

What emotions result?

There's a difference between how you feel about something and your emotions. Before you can change how you feel, you need to identify the emotion behind the feeling.

Examples of emotions: anger, joy, loneliness, anxiety, fear, happiness, and embarrassment (think about the emojis on your phone - they aren't feelings).

Examples of feelings: If you're angry, you may feel your muscles tense, your face turning red, or becoming flustered. On the other hand, when you're happy, your face lights up, your eyes sparkle, you smile and feel euphoric. You don't have a care in the world.

When you have your thoughts, beliefs, and emotions written down, you can validate what you are thinking and beliefs about the initial situation.

If something is not right, this gives you the opportunity to change it, especially from something negative to something positive.

THINKING ABOUT YOUR EMOTIONS WORKSHEET		
A	B	C
Situation	Belief	Emotion
What situations lead to your emotion?	What belief connects the situation and emotion?	What emotions result from the situation?

7 SIMPLE AND EFFECTIVE WAYS

TO BATTLE ANXIETY AND DEPRESSION WITHOUT MEDICATION

The Effective Strategies You Can Use on Your Own to Cope with Anxiety and Depression

Email RhondaJenkins786@gmail.com for your free copy

Rhonda Jenkins

Don't forget to email:
RhondaJenkins786@gmail.com
for your free copy of
The 7 Ways To Battle Anxiety

Chapter 4:

Your CBT Action Plan: Goal Setting for Success

"Success is peace of mind which is a direct result of self-satisfaction in knowing you did your best to become the best you are capable of becoming."

~ John Wooden

Now that you can recognize and identify some of your thought patterns, what can you do with them? When it comes to CBT, it's all about taking action. Some of the main goals of CBT are:

- To help improve your self-awareness and emotional intelligence by learning how to analyze your emotions, recognizing healthy emotions from unhealthy ones.
- Helping you reduce the negative impact of your current experiences as quickly as possible by investigating what's happening in situations right now. It's also focused on working and resolving problems you may be experiencing.
- Helping you to stop, or at least reduce further incidents causing you emotional pain. The aim is to allow you to grow as a person. CBT is based on helping you adjust your main beliefs. These beliefs are often the main reason for suffering the way that you do.
- Helping you understand why distorted thinking and perceptions can result in painful emotions.
- It teaches self-control through various techniques to help with thinking that may be distorted. CBT challenges this thinking.
- CBT teaches you that although you have no control over everything in this crazy world, we live in. You can control the way you look at things, understand things, and how you handle each situation that happens to you.
- CBT takes a structured approach and offers a recipe for this. You need to be prepared to be responsible and accountable to yourself, especially when you aren't working directly with a therapist.

The most important part of CBT on your part is being willing to make the changes necessary. You need to be accountable for your success or failure(s). One of the mistakes that people make is that they expect to read a book or see a therapist for one session, without putting the work in and expecting to get over the symptoms. It doesn't work like that. CBT is going to take time and effort, energy, and commitment on your part. That's not to say that it's doom and gloom. The success of CBT can be enjoyable at times. Focusing on the end goal—there is both light and hope at the end of the dark tunnel, which you may feel trapped in.

Work SMART, Not Hard

"Goals. There's no telling what you can do when you get inspired by them. There's no telling what you can do when you believe in them. And there's no telling what will happen when you act on them." ~ Jim Rohn

In the following section, we will go through how setting SMART goals is one of the best techniques to use. It's a proven method of goal setting that's systematic and easy to follow. The whole point of learning how is to make your life easier without becoming totally overwhelmed. There will be examples provided to make it simple to follow.

Before diving right into changing your thinking, making changes to your life, and developing new habits, you need to have a clear idea of exactly what you want to change. What would you like to see is that would be different from the life you're currently living?

In my personal experience, there were several thoughts and behaviors I really wanted to change. One of these was the guilt I was carrying around with me. It was only through this process that I could recognize that the guilt I was feeling was my husband's guilt. It had nothing to do with me. I chose to take this upon myself. It was serving me no purpose. Let's take a closer look at what SMART goals look like and how you can easily apply them to improve your own life.

SMART Goals

"People with clear, written goals, accomplish far more in a shorter period of time than people without them could ever imagine." ~ Brian Tracy

The word SMART is an acronym, where each letter in the word stands for a goal-setting component. When each of these points is properly defined, it becomes much easier to see your goals more clearly. They become clearly outlined for you to accomplish them. After all, what's the point of setting goals that are unrealistic or too difficult for you to achieve? All that you're likely to do in this case is to frustrate yourself. This will give you another reason for feeling additional guilt. Let's get started.

Specific

Your goals need to be clearly defined. You can't work toward something that's wishy-washy. Be clear about exactly what it is that you want. For example: Stop blaming myself for everyone else's mistakes.

Meaningful

Are the goals you set for yourself closely aligned with what you want to do and where you want to go? Sure, you want to improve yourself, but are these improvements going to make you a better person? Your goals need to be aligned with your personal beliefs and values. Anything less than this will hold you back and prevent you from really achieving whatever it is you want to achieve.

Achievable

Whatever goal you set for yourself needs to be something that you can achieve. Anything else will frustrate you and cause you to abandon the original goal you decided to work on.

Realistic

Are you being realistic about making the changes you've identified in your goal? Sometimes we set goals that are way below our capabilities, while other times we aim too high. Especially when it comes to mental health. Yes, you need to push yourself to grow, but you also need to know what your limitations are. Maybe you're not quite ready to take on a large goal. Always take this into consideration while you are setting your goal.

Timely

As with anything in life, things are measured in portions of time. When it comes to SMART goal setting, this is no different. You need to be clear about your start date as well as exactly when you would like to see the goal come to fruition. Once again, be realistic in your expectations. Let me tell you what happens when you don't have a timeline for your goals... You never see the result. Even if you don't fully reach your goal within your specified time frame, you can always set the same goal again (or those parts of your goal you still must achieve). There needs to be a specific start and end date to keep you motivated to work toward seeing the goal through to the end.

An example of a SMART goal would look something like this:

Specific – "I am going to get out at least once a week to overcome the anxiety and panic I feel out of the comfort of my home. I will do this for the next two months."

Meaningful – This goal is going to help you overcome anxiety and panic because it's going to force you to step outside of your comfort zone. At least once a week, you will need to think about different things you could be doing to expand your sense of safety and security. It's with the hope that you'll realize the world is not out to get you or a bad place.

Achievable – Initially, this goal may seem almost impossible for someone suffering from chronic panic attacks. However, working towards overcoming these fears by tackling one small thing at least once a week is achievable. There's no specific parameter set for this goal as to how long you need to get out. The point is to get out and away from the safety of your home.

Realistic – Is this something that you can do? Absolutely. You should start off small by doing it once a week. This can be built on in a future goal to set a time guideline or increase the frequency of when this needs to happen. The point is that you need to start off small.

Timely – You have put a time frame for your goal by stressing that you are going to do this for the next two months. The only thing you have forgotten is to add a start date. Here you could include "as of tomorrow" or "from Monday, (date)..." The important thing is to have both a start and end date as part of your goal.

So, what do you do if you don't meet your goal? One of the main things is to not make yourself feel any worse about it than you're already feeling. We all must fail at times. Remember that failure does not define you. You are worth way more than that.

When you're battling with one step in your goal setting and achievement process, go back to the section you are battling with and ask yourself whether the goal you have set yourself is too difficult right now. It's healthy to remember that you are working in a place that's challenging, without placing additional pressure on yourself. If this is the case, then maybe you need to break your goal down some more. Sometimes smaller steps are easier to accomplish, especially when you're just starting out.

Earlier, I mentioned that for real change to take place in CBT, you need to want to change. I might also add here that you need to feel ready to change as well. Don't give up—it's okay for you to go back to reassess your goals. Making a mistake or not quite reaching your goal is better than not trying at all. You should also avoid judging yourself or thinking negatively about it. You have more than enough to worry about instead of beating yourself up over goal setting as well.

If you've never worked with this type of goal setting before, then please know that this is going to take time to master. Imagine how great you'll feel about yourself each time you manage to achieve your goals? This is something that's necessary to help you build your self-esteem.

SMART Goal Exercise

When we're going through stress, anxiety, or depression, we often have no idea of where and how to start. The following worksheet may come in handy for you to work from. I have given you a good idea of what to focus on, above, but let's look at a manageable format for you to work with. Duplicate, or replicate this worksheet for each new goal. This will be easier for you to monitor and manage.

SMART GOALS WORKSHEET	
Specific	
Meaningful	
Achievable	
Realist	
Timely	
Notes	

Chapter 5:

Identifying Negative Thought Patterns

"Negativity, in general, is one of the things that holds people back, and you have to see what's holding you back to get away from it."

~ Lucy Dacus

When it comes to negative thinking and thought patterns, why do we have them?

Firstly, you need to understand that negative thoughts often occur without thinking about them. This happens automatically and is directly linked to things that happen to us throughout the day. There will always be situations that influence our thinking. Often, when we're in a bad place mentally, each of these thoughts is amplified, making them so much worse than they really are.

Some examples of negative thoughts might include:

- "I have the worst luck in the entire world. Why can't I just catch a break?"
- "I've just ruined my relationship. I will never find someone to love me."
- "She's running late and it's raining heavily. She has had an accident and her car is down an embankment somewhere."

These negative thoughts are examples of cognitive distortions. In CBT, we are taught that we develop this thinking as a means of dealing with negative life experiences. The longer we're subjected to bad experiences in our lives, the greater the chance that cognitive distortions will arise.

Types of Cognitive Distortions

Negative thinking results from thought patterns that are unreasonable, damaging to your internal beliefs about yourself, and that only adds to anxiety or depression you may already be feeling. According to cognitive behavioral therapy, these are known as cognitive distortions. Some examples of these include:

All or Nothing Thinking

Your thinking ends up drawing black or white conclusions about yourself with no gray areas in between. Whenever you find yourself thinking or using the words 'always' or 'never' in your thought process, you've moved into all or nothing thinking. Examples include: "I will never be as popular as Jane, she seems to have it all." "I always make the same mistakes doing spreadsheets, maybe I should just leave my job."

This type of thinking is common with those suffering from anxiety, panic attacks, depression, and other mental health issues. Unfortunately, thinking this way makes you sink deeper into despair because you can't see a way forward. You feel like the victim because it's all about how you've failed.

There is a way out, though. Becoming acutely aware of this type of thinking needs to happen before you can work on it. The reason for this is before you can get over it, you need to recognize when thinking negatively happens.

Stop seeing things as bad. Try to replace each negative thought with something positive about yourself. It will probably be hard to do at first, but with a little practice you can get it right. Instead of thinking everything about you is bad, remember your achievements, successes, and highs in your life. Be realistic. Everyone will go through times when things don't work out the way you want them to. Look for the silver lining and focus on the positive characteristics you have.

Stop dwelling on your weaknesses. Using negative terms that contain the words 'nothing,' or 'never,' should be banned from your thinking. If you can't help yourself from thinking this way, it may be helpful to speak with trusted friends or family members. They can help you see all the good things you have to offer. It's worth gaining another perspective, especially a positive one.

Discounting the Positive

They automatically assume that positive statements made to them, or positive situations aren't genuine. Often this is because they don't believe they are worthy of anything good. Words to look out for when discounting the positive are things like luck,' 'by chance,' or 'accidentally.' They might say things like: "I was just lucky..." or "The only reason the shop assistant was nice to me is that it's their job."

They believe anything good that happens to them has nothing to do with anything they've done. Everything is in the hands of circumstances, in which they have no control over what happens to them. This results in feeling demotivated, and helpless.

Emotional Reasoning

Here, you might believe your thoughts and emotions are real. Nothing can be further from the truth. For instance, you may believe you're overweight. No matter how many people tell you how good you look, you believe your own thinking. If you think you are fat, then surely it must be true.

Paying attention to emotions is important, however, each of these thoughts should be analyzed and validated. Question each of these emotions. Try and find where the emotion comes from. What proof do you have that your thinking is correct? Has someone else confirmed this to support your emotions? Can you support your thinking with facts?

You may be more inclined to think this way if you suffer from anxiety or depression.

Jumping to Conclusions

This is a common thought distortion. You seldom have all the facts at your disposal. Instead of questioning your thinking, you automatically make your own assumptions. If someone happens to be short or abrupt with you, you assume it has something to do with you. Maybe you said or did something to make them behave this way toward you. Nine times out of ten, they are probably upset about something completely unrelated that has nothing to do with you.

You spend your time stewing over their behavior, trying to put your finger on reasons for their behavior. Here, you are trying to mind-read, instead of thinking rationally. If you can't think of anything you may have said or done, then chances are you've made an incorrect assumption. Holding grudges that aren't necessary can destroy friendships and relationships with others. Are you prepared to sacrifice these relationships based on believing that you know what the other person is thinking?

Labeling

When a situation happens, you may take this to the extreme and label everything and everyone according to the singular event. Just because someone happens to be sad for a couple of days, they are automatically labeled a miserable person. Another example of distorted thinking when it comes to labeling is if a friend happens to pass you in the street without greeting. You automatically label them as being snobbish, or angry with you. They may have been deep in thought, or just not seen you. Placing a label on the situation isn't healthy. Your thoughts are irrational and inaccurate.

You may even choose to label yourself or others with labels that aren't true. Think of some of the negative labels you've given yourself... Maybe you believe you're 'aggressive,' 'a failure,' 'unapproachable,' 'an alcoholic,' or 'stupid.' Take care not to label those around you either. Let's face it, labels can easily destroy relationships.

Magnification and Minimization

Maximization and minimization are two sides of the same coin. It's making way more of a situation than it needs to be or making something important seem less than what it is. Another way of looking at this is exaggerating whatever has happened and blowing it off or blowing it out of proportion. Think about a personal achievement that you've worked hard to earn. Instead of accepting the recognition you deserve, you minimize it by saying "It was nothing really."

Mental Filters

This thinking causes you to only see things in a negative light. It's the inability to see or accept that the world has many good things in it. Instead of rose-tinted glasses, yours are blackened out where all you can see is darkness. You settle for a glass half-empty outlook on life. Through distorted thinking, you can understand how those suffering from panic attacks choose to avoid social interaction at all costs. They have convinced themselves that there's nothing good for them out there.

Another form of distorted thinking negatively influences depression and anxiety. If you sit back and look at things realistically and can understand that the opposite to white is black, then it also stands to reason that negativity has an opposite as well—positivity. Happiness is the opposite of sadness. Hope versus hopelessness. Sunlight rather than the darkness of night.

Overgeneralizing

When you make a general assumption about something based on one or two events. Things might just be coincidental, but you take this as fact. You're prepared to jump to conclusions about situations and apply this to all events. Although we've already used this example, it's worth mentioning again, being rubbish at working with spreadsheets does not make you totally useless. Yes, you may have a weakness that needs a bit of work. This can be overcome irrespective of the thoughts you may have now.

The two disorders most affected by overgeneralization are anxiety disorders as well as post-traumatic stress (PTSD). This is just another thought distortion that just causes you to be miserable.

Personalization and Blame

When you allow an event or situation from your past to dictate how you act or react today. It's assuming the blame for things that aren't your fault. You continue to beat yourself up about things that may have happened in your childhood or over something you had no control over. An example of this would be if your parents divorced when you were still quite young. All these years you've been carrying guilt around with you that maybe if you had behaved better, they wouldn't have fought so much and got divorced.

Can you see how unrealistic this thinking is? Your parents' divorce had nothing to do with you. Sure, you have been affected by it, but they probably take you into consideration each step of the way. However, their decision wasn't based on anything you did wrong.

Maybe you haven't been invited to attend a function. Immediately, you assume the worst. You believe that the decision was made deliberately to hurt you. Of course, when you're suffering from depression or anxiety, all this is going to do is make these conditions worse. Unrelated events are incorrectly personalized, and we incorrectly accept blame.

'Should' Statements

These are statements that they make to themselves, or about the behavior that follows these unrealistic beliefs and expectations. They set unattainable goals and conditions for themselves. This could relate to values, and beliefs. There's only one result from self-berating talk and that's adding to anxiety and panic. It is having the exact opposite effect on them to their goal with CBT. Words used in these sentences include things like 'ought to have,' or 'should have.'

This negative thinking has been learned even from childhood. Imagine having your parents, teachers, or those closest to you telling you that you can never succeed. Although this may have been said to you as a child, the scars and beliefs are still there. It only serves to make you blind to anything good in your life. The result: your self-esteem takes a hammering.

Cognitive Distortions

Discounting the Positive

'SHOULD' STATEMENTS

Emotional Reasoning

All or Nothing Thinking

Overgeneralizing

Magnification and Minimization

Labelling

Jumping to Conclusions

Mental Filters

Personalization and Blame

What Thought is Causing the Feeling

All thoughts must originate somewhere. When you understand a thought is triggering anxiety or bringing your mood down, the first step is to identify the distorted thinking taking place. There are ten common thought distortions above for you to choose from as you begin to identify your thoughts. Are you guilty of magnification or minimization, emotional reasoning, all-or-nothing thinking? Maybe there are others that resonate with you instead. Whatever you think you are guilty of, give it a label. Recognize it for what it is without trying to justify why you're thinking this way.

According to a psychotherapist, and author of 13 Things mentally strong people don't do: Take back your power, embrace change, face your fears, and train your brain for happiness and success (2017), Amy Morin says:

"What you think directly influences how you feel and how you behave. So, if you think you're a failure, you feel like a failure. Then, you'll act like a failure, which reinforces your belief that you must be a failure." (Morin, 2016).

Mentally, you choose to reinforce your thinking by justifying why you think the way you do. No matter if there is evidence to the contrary, you will believe what you want to believe. Anything else gets disregarded. However, just as we discussed in the opening chapters of this book, there's no such thing as a magic bullet to get rid of all negativities through the power of positive thinking. Positive thinking can lead to behaving in a more positive way, which can improve your outlook on life, but it won't solve any of your mental health disorders.

There are a couple of ways for you to identify what you are feeling, (your emotions). While we'd like to think that each of our thought patterns happens in isolation from one another, this is simply not the case. It can be done to a degree, mind you, but this is going to take a lot of practice and pay extremely close attention to your thinking than ever before. Right now, our thoughts are racing all over the place.

You can't seem to help waking up and thinking about having a nice warm cup of coffee to start your day just right. You're also thinking about the dog that needs to go outside, the dishes in the dishwasher that need to be put away, that presentation you need to do at the office at your early morning team meeting. Is there anything more you need to add? Is it going to sound boring? What am I going to wear? Is it bold enough? Will I make a business statement? I wonder what traffic is going to be like on the freeway. Hopefully, you won't be late. The manager hates tardiness.

Running out the door, you try and mentally recall whether you have everything you should have done. Did you close and lock each of the windows in the house? Does the dog have enough food? Maybe I should just go and check on the house, just once more before I leave...

This is an example of just how many thoughts we may experience within a space of about 30 minutes. The big question now is how many of these thoughts are realistic, how many of them are on the spectrum of being over-the-top or just plain creepy. Can you see how this thinking can negatively affect you and make your life as miserable as hell? The solution to this is to carefully consider and be aware of what you are thinking. Do these thoughts add to your happiness, or are they adding to your levels of stress, frustration (with yourself and your circumstances,) and even anxiety? This process should happen more than once a day. It needs to become part of your daily routine. Those thoughts that are worthwhile and productive should be kept and added on, while negative ones should be done away with.

Other ways that these emotions influence how we behave (this becomes a continuous cycle):

- One of the results of emotion affects actions we take in treating ourselves and those around us either positively or negatively.
- Unhealthy cycles begin and begin to flourish.
- Next up, it results in how we think. Are our thoughts logical or irrational? These thoughts will determine our behavior.

We must be able to identify which of our thoughts are positive or negative. Part of the process is calling out all negative thinking and all the unnecessary things we fill our minds with each day. Allowing your mind to wander, unchecked can cause dangerous behavior. For example, you're so busy thinking about the presentation you need to do at this morning's meeting that you don't see another car turning into your lane at the same time as you. Thank goodness you come to your senses quickly enough and can avoid a collision. This may have been a very close shave, however, unless you can control what you are thinking and when these close calls may one day be more serious.

Maybe you use some of these ways to handle the stress and anxiety you're going through:

- Taking drugs, alcohol, over-the-counter medication, and even prescribed medicine excessively. Some of these behaviors could have serious consequences and do very little to change the situation you are in.
- Rely on those around you for support, no matter how hard, or uncomfortable this may be at first. Never be too proud to ask for help, especially when you are feeling at the lowest point in your life.
- A lack of emotional intelligence can negatively influence our relationships. The reality is that unless you can love and tolerate yourself, how do you expect to open your heart to others?

So, how can you regain control over this?

One of the ways is to identify your emotions, especially how they are connected to what you're going through. Maybe you feel like a failure because your application for a promotion at work was turned down. The emotion here is feeling like a failure. The situation is that you never received the promotion... This may lead to not wanting to go to work, losing interest in what you're supposed to be doing, or deciding to look for another job. Do you see how just one negative thought can lead to irrational behavior?

To come to terms with our thoughts and feelings, we should be able to tell the difference between random, automatic thoughts, and deliberate thinking. In the section above, 'Mental Filters,' we've discussed how the brain can sort through our thinking to focus on what's important and what's not.

Make a list in your journal or on a blank sheet of paper of each of the thoughts you have throughout the day. This is one of the few ways you will get to the bottom of which thoughts you are having and how they affect your emotions and behavior. We need to learn to sift out unnecessary thinking to make way for thinking that is necessary.

One technique that can help you come to terms with some of the negative thoughts that plague your mind constantly is known as the 'five-minute triple column technique'. First introduced by clinical psychiatrist, Dr David Burns, author of Feeling Great: The revolutionary new treatment for depression and anxiety (2020). As the name suggests, all this exercise takes is five minutes a day. While most of us complain about the fact we don't have enough time during the day as it is, I'm sure that if you know this is going to help alleviate some of the stress, anxiety, and pressure you're facing each day, you'll happily be prepared to sacrifice something to find this tiny block of time.

It may be worth going back and re-reading the 10 cognitive distortions that you might experience. It's okay to practice this technique whenever you're feeling one of these cognitive distortions or at the same time every day.

Divide your piece of paper, or journal page, into three equal columns. Label the first column, 'Negative Auto-thinking.' You know that little voice in your head that keeps telling you that you're a 'failure,' 'you are fat,' 'stupid,' 'ugly,' 'mean,' 'unpopular,' or whatever other bad belief you seem to have adopted during the day. Beneath each automatic thought, write a brief description of why you feel this way today. One of the reasons for doing this is so you can physically see these thoughts in front of you, written down. Sometimes, this can be sobering. An example of a statement attached to one of these thoughts could be:

"I'm unpopular because nobody asked for my opinion during the morning meeting. I should have stepped in to defend myself, but I'm too slow and stupid for that."

In the second column, connect this thought with cognitive distortion as listed above. For the example above, cognitive distortions might include:

- all-or-nothing thinking
- jumping to conclusions
- overgeneralization
- personalization, blame, and
- should statements

Can you see that several cognitive distortions can be linked to a single thought? Your initial response is certainly flawed. In the final column, make a note of the same thought(s) if you look at it rationally... This could now look like this.

"Although nobody asked for my opinion during the morning meeting, I knew I could voice my opinion as I had done many times before. Not having something to say doesn't make me a bad person."

Can you see how this completely changes how your thoughts are interpreted? Not only that, but I'm sure that, given a similar situation, you'll be able to weigh up all the options before jumping to a negative conclusion.

Example of the five minute triple column technique

Negative Auto-thinking	Why do I feel this way today?	What is the cognitive distortion?

Useful Questions

- Why is keeping a thought record important?
- When is the best time to note these thoughts?
- How can we catch negative thoughts that fall under negative thinking?
- How are you experiencing your thoughts? Through negative self-talk (that voice inside your head that won't shut up?)
- Do you see yourself failing in images, or do you imagine what others might be saying behind your back?

The best time to make a note of what you're thinking is immediately the thought crosses your mind. This is how we can catch ourselves thinking about them. This is the easiest way to work through each of these thoughts.

You can answer each of these questions by writing them down with your answer(s) alongside them.

As a brief reminder of what we've covered in this chapter. Firstly, it required quite a bit of action on your part. It encourages you to take some time to identify your negative thoughts. We've gone through 10 different cognitive distortions that can influence our thinking. Finally, we've focused on why it's important to keep a record of the thoughts you experience daily.

Chapter 6:

Transforming Negative Thought Patterns

"Just as negative beliefs at some point entered your subconscious mind, and began to subtly shape your lives, new, positive beliefs can also be "planted" there: beliefs that will gradually begin to improve your behavior, your thinking, the way you feel, and thus, your life."

~ David Bolton

While we briefly touched on some ways to change our negative thought patterns at the end of Chapter 4, in this chapter we are going to look at this in-depth. There are plenty of reasons why you should be doing this. In Chapter 4, you will find content to help you see reality rather than trying to get you to think 'positively.' It's focused on changing the beliefs you have about yourself. You may want to refer to the worksheet you completed at the end of Chapter 2. This will remind you of the very close connection between our thoughts, beliefs, and behavior are interlinked.

Thought distortions only add more pressure to any of the mental health disorders you may be experiencing presently. Think about it, thinking negatively won't increase or improve your self-esteem. All it's going to do is further break down how you are already feeling about yourself. As we work through this chapter, you will learn how to change cognitive distortions and how to replace these with new, and positive beliefs.

CBT doesn't focus on making you 'think happy thoughts' to get rid of negative thinking. It goes deeper than that. The purpose of CBT is to sift through the noise and find what's real. It's viewing the present in the here and now. What is your current reality?

There will be some further questions to ask yourself, as well as another worksheet.

According to traditional CBT, you should be able to be sure your current thinking is true. What proof do you have that what you're thinking is correct? Are there reasons why your thinking could be distorted?

Here are several ways to analyze your thinking to see what's right and what may be completely off base.

- We need to be able to defend our thoughts
- Find proof to back up the way you are thinking
- Is there anything contrary to this thinking?

CBT influences our thinking in the following ways:

- Thoughts grounded in common sense. Things that most people are already aware of because they're so commonplace. An example of this would be that if you touch a hot stovetop, there's a high probability that you are going to burn your fingers.

To put it into simpler terms:

You have an image of something in mind. This has a cause-and-effect relationship. For every action, there must be an accompanying reaction, and our choice of action or reaction will determine the outcome.

Apart from having a specific image in mind, maybe it's an incident that takes place where emotions are involved. A close work colleague passes you while shopping without acknowledging you. Immediately you assume that there must be something wrong with you that they didn't bother to greet you. Maybe you've done something to offend them, and that's why they're ignoring you. You spend the rest of the day stewing over it. You run different scenarios in your head, scanning memories from the past, trying to figure out what you did wrong. All the while driving yourself insane. The truth is way simpler—your colleagues may have just had a lot on their minds and weren't paying close attention to what was happening around them. It begs the question though, why didn't you make a point of greeting them?

Thank goodness we are different. Can you imagine how boring the world would be if we were all the same? We have different features, different characteristics, different personalities, and preferences. Along with this, we each feel emotions completely differently. What may bother me, may not be important for you. The problem with this, of course, is that we each interpret different signs, cues, verbal, and non-verbal communication differently. What someone else may shrug off as being unimportant may really get to you, making you even more anxious or depressed than usual. You may not think that this is so important, but the way we try and understand what's happening around us makes a difference.

It's interesting that not even identical twins will experience the same emotions or attitude toward a situation or experience.

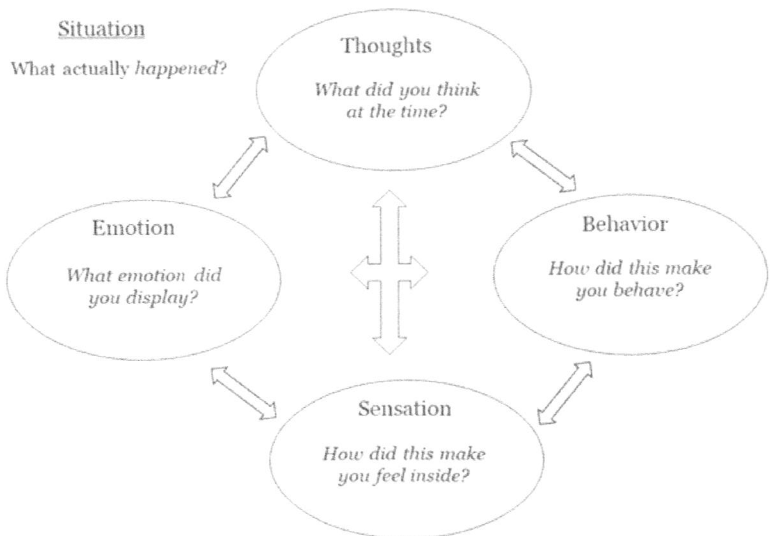

Interpretation Diagram Example

Interpretation is Important

Because each of us is unique, one of us may see each new situation as an opportunity to learn something and grow. Another may see the situation as one of the biggest challenges ever faced. Emotions of doubt about their abilities and the situation in general result in despair and desperation. In this example, one thing is sure, both parties have aligned themselves with their feelings.

According to the best-selling author of Man's search for Meaning (1949/2006) who survived the death camps in Germany during the second world war, Viktor Frankl stated:

"Everything can be taken from a man but one thing: the last of human freedom – to choose one's attitude in any given set of circumstances, to choose one's own way."

Using Common Sense as a Guide

These are day-to-day events, situations, and things you don't even need to think about because they happen automatically. You know that even after the darkest night, the dawn will break and a brand-new day will arrive, allowing us to begin again with a whole new set of opportunities.

Common things that we take for granted, but we know we can rely on are things like gravity. You know for sure that if you knock a coffee mug off a tall counter, it's likely to shatter into several pieces. We've got accustomed to flicking on a light switch and having the entire room lit up. None of these day-to-day automatic behaviors require any form of emotion. This behavior is automated. Each of these activities has the same results. There's no need to even think about an outcome. While these are just a couple of examples, think about things you do, experience in your daily life, or on a regular basis that falls under the 'common sense' category.

So, we can retain our unique individuality, it's important that we have the freedom to be able to think on our own, interpret each situation as and when it occurs, and decide how to behave.

What Are You Thinking?

To grip our emotions, we need to be able to understand the difference between our core and intermediate beliefs, and automatic thoughts. Before we can really get into this, we need to first understand what is meant by each of these terms:

Core Beliefs

Those things we believe about who we are, who others are, and the world in which we live. It's our beliefs right to the very 'core.' This is also where most of our negative thoughts come from. Many of these beliefs have been formed since we were much younger. These have possibly been molded and shaped by dominant figures in our early lives.

This is not to say that because you were taught something as a child you need to continue believing in the same thing(s) even as an adult. Surely, you have formed your own opinion on situations and circumstances. The problem is that all too often we are still living in the past and sticking to incorrect values and traditions without trying to validate them for ourselves. We've become stuck. Because we're stuck, we're also not open to accepting new concepts and ideas, no matter how flawed our beliefs may be.

Intermediate Beliefs

Instead of taking on someone else's ideas, as with core beliefs, these are beliefs and attitudes that you decide to apply in all situations. In many ways, it's like generalizing and treating each situation the same. Remember I mentioned that we are each different and unique? Well, this is an excellent example of where someone stuck with flawed intermediate beliefs could become stuck. They're not prepared to give an inch.

An example of this is when you may have had a cheating spouse. An intermediate belief would be that "all women/men can't be trusted because they all cheat." Of course, this could not be further from the truth. Sure, there are those who do, but that's not to say that everyone can be given the same negative label.

Automatic Thoughts

As the name would indicate, you may not even be aware that your mind and thoughts are going somewhere else. Because these thoughts often sneak up on you, unless you're wide awake and paying attention to every single thought, chances are you'll miss them. There's a sure way to be able to pay closer attention to where each of your thoughts is taking you and how they are influencing your subsequent behavior. In the following worksheet, we are going to work through ways for you to become acutely aware of what you're thinking and how this affects your situation, your behavior, and your emotions.

Thought Record

In the attached worksheet, you will see that this has been divided into two columns and six lines. The purpose of this worksheet is for you to be able to identify and record each of your thoughts. Especially those that appear automatically, or randomly.

The first row has been filled with an example that should explain how to use this worksheet.

Line One:

Identify the situation that sets the thoughts in motion.

- When did you first notice that your thoughts had shifted about a situation?
- The secret to using the first column is to list as many things as possible that you can remember about the situation.
- Think about where you were, did something happen that made you suddenly think or remember this experience?
- Was there a 'trigger', and if so, what was it?
- Were you with someone, did they have anything to do with the thought?
- Were you doing something specific?

Line Two:

Here, the focus is on the emotions or feelings you may have experienced because of column one. Often this can be described using single words, for example sadness, anger, hopelessness—you get the picture. It's important that you complete this section as you need to rely on each line being filled in for the final line to make sense.

- In one word, describe exactly what emotion you felt.
- On a scale of 0 to 100, how strong was the emotion? With 0 being not strong at all, and 100 being overwhelming.
- What was going on physically in your body? How did your body react? Maybe you were trembling uncontrollably, or you suddenly began crying—these reactions are different from one person to the next.

Line Three:

They're automatic, so they may be a bit more difficult to spot. You may be so used to them by now that you hardly even notice they're there. Automatic thoughts can be described as thoughts that randomly enter your mind against your will.

- How many of these thoughts are negative?
- Are these thoughts judging what's happening now, or things that have occurred in the past?
- Do these automatic thoughts include other people? If so, who?
- Are these actual thoughts, or images? Are you experiencing memories of the past or possibly even flashbacks?
- Can you say what was going through your mind just before you started thinking this way? Maybe you overheard someone speaking about the subject, or you read something that suddenly triggered an automatic thought?
- Can you put a timeline for the thought, situation, or event? Is it something that happened recently, in your childhood, or because of an event in your life?

A great example might be seeing yourself paralyzed now just thinking about having to face a crowd of people in a shopping center. You suffer from claustrophobia, and too many people only make these feelings worse.

Line Four:

Test the thought—Between this line and the next, you need to be able to argue your case behind the thought.

What proof or argument do you have that could possibly support your thinking?

Is it something that's genuine and realistic?

Line Five:

Is there any reason for you to doubt whether this thinking is flawed? Take into consideration that this thought may be automatic, negative, and destructive.

Line Six:

Study lines four and five carefully. Weigh each of the options from these lines, taking all factors into consideration. What is in favor of the thought, what supports it, and what will make you place the thought under a microscope while you question its validity. What is your conclusion? Be careful that no cognitive bias exists.

Thought Record Worksheet		

One of the benefits of making use of this thought record is to change the way you're currently thinking and develop entirely new thoughts. Here are some examples of what these brand-new thoughts can look like:

Old thought – "I'm too ugly for anyone to love me."

New thought – "I have many qualities and characteristics that someone will love."

Old thought – "I must have done something wrong because my friend didn't greet me."

New thought – "We are such good friends; I wonder if they're maybe going through something. Maybe I can help in some way."

Notice how each of the new thoughts is longer than old thoughts and make a positive statement rather than focusing on the negative. This is where you want to get to by questioning each of your negative thoughts. Bring them into focus and validate whether they are real. If they aren't then it's worth replacing them with things that you know for a fact are true.

Another quick way of getting to this is by asking yourself the following questions:

Is there credible evidence to support my thought(s)?

What credible evidence is there against the thoughts I'm having?

In addition to these, you can also ask yourself some of the following questions that are supposedly thanks to the work of the ancient philosopher Socrates. Very few records of this great contributor's work were left behind at his death in 399 B.C. The teaching and writing we do have are thanks to one of Socrates' students, Plato. As a teacher and philosopher, Socrates believed that it was better for his students to learn by becoming inquisitive and asking deep questions. Many teachers of the time were prepared to bombard their students with information in the hopes that they would be able to retain this information.

Socrates believed in asking the following five types of questions. In doing so, he laid the foundation for questioning techniques that have been used by counselors, and therapists for many years, especially in CBT. The purpose of this type of questioning technique is to remove all vague questions that really don't add value to your thought process and replace them with those that do. Before we get down to these questions, it's being able to ask questions that are open-ended. Let's look at the difference between closed questions and open-ended questions quickly. A close-ended question is one where you can answer with a simple 'Yes' or 'No'. On the other hand, open-ended questions make you really think about your answer(s).

Socratic Questioning in Detail

Let me ask you this... How many times have you really thought about the types of questions you're asking? Are they worthwhile? Do they make you think about what's going on in your life right now, what's happened in the past, and what you'd like to see in the future? In the words of Socrates himself:

"I know you won't believe me, but the highest form of human excellence is to question oneself and others." ~ Socrates

Using the following questions can help us not only understand the way we're thinking, but also the way others see us and how we see them. As part of this technique,

To define Socratic questioning techniques, we need to cover each of the following five things:

Be sure that you are clear about the meaning behind your thoughts.

What emotions are you feeling that are connected to these thoughts?

If you keep thinking this way, what consequences will happen?

Where does this perception of your thoughts come from?

Does another type of thought exist that will result in a different outcome?

Notice how each of these questions makes you really think about each answer. It's not good enough to just be able to answer, 'yes' or 'no', especially when each of your thoughts may be distorted.

Are your thoughts reasonable, or irrational? What I mean by this is whether you are taking all the facts into consideration, or whether most of these thoughts aren't based on facts that you can prove.

How often has your mind been invaded by specific thoughts and you question whether everyone else thinks the same as you do? The truth is that none of us think the same way. Each of us is unique in our own right. At any given moment, we may be thinking about the past, present, or future. While CBT isn't focused on the past, it certainly works with the present moment if experiences from the past are currently appearing on your radar now and they're holding you back.

If you battle with anxiety or depression, you know firsthand how destructive and debilitating this thinking can be. They manage to suck the very joy out of life, leaving you feeling miserable and vulnerable to other intrusive thoughts and beliefs. It's easy for you to waste your time wallowing in self-pity—maybe because nobody else is prepared to pay attention to you when you're in this way.

Thoughts can overwhelm you unless you can find a way to cope that's effective and works for you. Let's look at some patterns of irrational thinking. These thoughts:

- They are founded on things that have happened in the past. It doesn't matter whether these experiences are negative, or positive.
- Cannot be backed by any evidence. No matter how hard you try, you simply cannot find any proof that these thoughts are true.
- Most of your thoughts are supported by things you assume to be true, rather than things you know to be true. There is a distinct difference between the assumptions and the truth.

How can you be your own best friend? When you think of a best friend, it would be someone you know will always be there to back you up. They can be used as a sounding board when you want to discuss things that are important to you. Sometimes they stop you from doing some crazy stuff by putting things into perspective for you. You know they are reliable. They give you great advice. In most instances, they love you unconditionally, just as you are.

So, what if you had to be this person for yourself? We waste so much time being hard on ourselves. Would your self-talk be different if you questioned whether you would speak to your best friend that way? What would you do differently? Chances are you would never be all that hard on them because you value them and your friendship too much. You won't run them down to others or spend your time looking for ways to sabotage them.

Maybe you need to consider putting yourself first. Pretending that you're your own best friend. This may make you look at yourself in a different light.

Chapter 7:

How-to Guide to Face Fears and Manage Stress and Anxiety

"Fear keeps us focused on the past or worried about the future. If we can acknowledge our fear, we can realize that right now we are okay. Right now, today, we are still alive, and our bodies are working marvelously. Our eyes can still see the beautiful sky. Our ears can still hear the voices of our loved ones."

~ Thich Nhat Hahn (n.d.)

Have you ever had something you're so afraid is going to harm you, where your fear is so real that you can't seem to focus on anything else? You may have a long list of things you're terrified of. While some people may find some of your fear's irrational and unnecessary, the important thing is that they are very real in your own mind.

These fears could possibly be the result of something that's happened in the past or even experiences you have in the present.

We've already discussed that fear hormones have been around for centuries, and this is what acts as a protection mechanism to keep us safe from genuine threats. What about all the other phobias that are offshoots from fear? These have the power to restrict our lives, effectively making us slaves and trapping us in a fear loop. The more we think about the thing(s) we fear, the worse these become for us.

The strange thing about fear is that it may be a real threat that we're afraid of, or it could be something we've only ever imagined in our minds. This is especially true when we experience panic disorders. Just for a moment, stop and think rationally, and realistically.

The main driving force in your brain for most panic disorders is that others (out there) are trying to get you and to cause you harm. Can you recognize the flaws in this thinking? Sure, there is a hell of a lot of people out there and not all of them are touchy-feely individuals who will give you warm fuzzies. However, it's highly unlikely that your fear of others is because, in your mind, there are people lurking behind each corner, bush, and passageway with the explicit agenda of harming you.

Apart from panic disorders, let's look at some of the other phobias and fears that may be holding you back and preventing you from living the life you deserve.

Phobias literally paralyze you. The root word for phobia comes from a Greek word that literally means "fear of horror" (O'Keefe Osborn, Legg, 2019). There are so many phobias that you could be petrified of. Some of these include:

- The opposite of dealing with crowds is finding yourself completely alone. This phobia is known as acrophobia.
- Crowds—claustrophobia can be the cause of you being afraid to confront many people, especially in a confined space. You may especially be wary of climbing into elevators because the sheer thought of being stuck in a box if the elevator breaks down is more than you can handle.
- Heights—acrophobia. This may have been caused by a tall uncle placing you on his shoulders as a toddler and pretending to drop you. Of course, this never happened, but the memory is still deeply ingrained in your psyche.
- Injections or hospitals—hemophobia, this is more the fear of blood. For some people, they can't even watch blood being drawn without feeling woozy. Not a great feeling at all, especially in times of emergency.
- Water, as in hydrophobia. This water doesn't even really need to be deep. Some individuals with hydrophobia won't even swim in a small pool of water.

When it comes to phobias, there is a really long list of items, and situations that one may or may not be afraid of... Most of these phobias require extensive work in CBT. While there is work necessary, it's not impossible to get a handle on these phobias and to even overcome them.

Facing Your Fears - Exposure Therapy

Psychologists and therapists make use of something known as "Exposure Therapy" to face these fears and phobias head-on. They've found that this technique is especially effective when treating various phobias, stress, anxiety, and post-traumatic stress disorder (PTSD).

It's almost a natural reaction for you to want to avoid those things, people, or situations that you're afraid of, or maybe they make you feel uncomfortable. In exposure therapy, the exact opposite occurs. Therapy wants you to become comfortable with the very thing(s) that are making you feel uncomfortable. If it's people, it's getting you to begin socializing with a group of people that you're familiar with. They should be able to comfort you, reassuring you that you're in a safe place and that nothing untoward is going to happen. Next, you may be introduced to a situation where there are a few strangers to get you into the habit of being around strangers.

Guided exposure lets you increase your levels of exposure to your fears and phobias in such a way that you control the narrative. You will also learn how to recognize and cope with any triggers as and when they happen. During this process, you need to pay close attention to your emotions, how they are being influenced, and whether you're able to handle additional exposure to your phobias or not.

When we don't do anything about these phobias, they lead to extreme anxiety and increased fear. The ultimate result of this could very well be depression. All the things you're trying to avoid.

How will you know you're Suffering from Anxiety?

Here are some of the most common symptoms that indicate that you may experience anxiety. The reality is that no matter who you are, at some point in your life, you're going to experience anxiety in some form or another. While it may just be temporary, given your situation, it's the long-term anxiety we're referring to here. The type of anxiety that seems to surround you and wants to suffocate you with fear.

Agitation

A great part of this relates to our primitive brains. We begin to shake, sweat, and can't control our heart rate, which feels like it's going through the roof. It's believing that there's something dangerous close by, or about to happen and you have no control over it. This is where the fight-or-flight mode kicks in. The problem is that if you are prone to anxiety disorder, it's going to take you quite a while before these feelings goes away. You'll battle to pull yourself back to normal. Your mind and body will remain at high alert.

Fatigue

This may seem confusing as most people associate anxiety with being restless, and excitable. Think about how exhausted you feel once you've experienced a panic, or anxiety attack? For others, being tired for no reason could be constant. This might be because of difficulties sleeping, where your body is simply not getting the rest it needs, or because your body is aching from tense muscles (all symptoms of a long-term anxiety disorder). Being tired all the time could also be an underlying symptom of depression. It's worth monitoring this to be sure that your symptoms aren't worse than they should be.

Irrational Fears

We've just spoken about fears and phobias. These would fall under irrational fears. It's being afraid of something, someone, or a situation that's not only out of the ordinary but unrealistic. We've also gone through ways of working through some of these fears using the exposure technique. The sooner you can get this under control, the sooner you'll be able to scratch this off of your symptoms list that's contributing to your anxiety.

Irritability

You become irritated by the least little thing, all the time. This could lead to you being short, abrupt, and quick to lose your temper. In most instances, this is the least little thing.

Panic Attacks and Avoiding Social Situations

Another two symptoms are closely linked to one another. Actual symptoms of a panic attack include an increased heart rate, nausea, shortness of breath, a tight chest, trembling, and sweating. Panic attacks can happen without warnings. It's difficult to identify the exact trigger that's likely to set this off. The biggest challenge with panic attacks and anxiety is that they're difficult to control and happen often enough to be a real problem.

Restlessness

This is normally found in teenagers, although it can also be experienced by adults. You feel that you need to move on. You can't explain why, it's just a feeling that you have. Don't use this as a definite symptom to diagnose anxiety, because not everyone with an anxiety disorder displays this as a symptom.

Tense Muscles

Constantly, battling with muscle tension may be a visible symptom of anxiety disorder. There's no clear relationship between why you battle with tension in your body. It's believed that tense muscles add to feelings of anxiety.

Trouble Concentrating

For me, this is finding it hard to connect the dots. I battle to focus on things for long periods of time. Decision-making is impaired (or at least much slower than usual). It seems to affect short-term memory rather than long-term. You know, when you must ask the same things a couple of times in the space of a few days. Those around you can become quite irritated having to give you the same answer time after time. You need to explain to them that this is one of the symptoms of a general anxiety disorder (GAD).

This symptom is also linked to poor or at least a decrease in what was once excellent performance. This behavior isn't intentional, of course, it's literally a symptom of battling with anxiety.

Trouble Falling Asleep

Insomnia and restless sleep are both common symptoms of anxiety. Closely linked to fatigue due to a lack of sleep, it's quite important to treat each of these symptoms. Many issues with anxiety can be traced back to these vital symptoms. Consider how this influences most of your life? If you can't sleep, or your sleep is restless, you battle to function. You suffer from feelings of fatigue, which in turn can lead to irritability. This can impair your ability to concentrate and make rational decisions. And so on... Can you see how these two symptoms can have so many negative effects on any anxiety disorder?

Unnecessary Worry

This is literally worrying about every little thing. It's becoming so focused on something that will probably never happen, or someone that will never do what you're worried about. You can consider this anxiety disorder if these feelings continue for six months or more. If you simply can't control these emotions, chances are you need to work through them. Your thinking is so out of control that you battle to function normally.

FEAR: Face Everything and Recover

While it may not feel like it right now, there are ways to deal with and work through fears you may be experiencing, anxiety, and even panic attacks. If you can quite get over them immediately, you can make a start and through CBT work consistently to cope with the symptoms you have right now.

Although anxiety and fear are often combined and classified as two sides of the same coin, they are quite different from one another. Fear happens when something is tangible and understood. Think of fear of heights or snakes. You know that if you're at the top of an eight-story building, it's high when you're standing on the roof. You also know that the Amazon is full of a multitude of slimy, slithering reptiles that may or may not be extremely toxic and harmful to humans and other animals. You may never have had a run-in with a snake before, but you just don't like them. Each of these things is real. You can see them, touch them, and they're easy to understand.

Anxiety, on the other hand, is fear of the unknown. A noise could startle you. The big question is whether you know for certain what it is... Chances are that you may think you know, but you can't be certain. Maybe you're feeling uneasy because you believe someone's following you. You begin to feel anxious about this. Your body begins to display all the physical symptoms associated with anxiety. You're not 100% positive that you really do have a stalker after you. For all you know, it may just be another pedestrian who happens to be walking in the same general direction as you are. Anxiety drives you crazy with things that are unknown. Although similar, they aren't the same.

Some Symptoms of Anxiety are:

- Battling to breathe
- Combination of hot and cold flushes
- Diarrhea
- Feeling dizzy
- Feeling tense, especially in your muscles
- Headaches
- Increased heart rate
- Nausea
- Pain in your chest that can't be explained
- Problems sleeping
- Questioning your own sanity
- Ringing in your ears
- Sweating profusely
- Tingling sensation in hands and/or feet
- Unexplained tremors or shaking
- Wanting to faint

Notice how these symptoms differ from these identified of fear. Most of these are the same, but notice that anxiety has more symptoms than the following:

- Battling to breathe
- Hot and cold flushes
- Increased heartbeat

- The mouth is constantly dry
- Nausea
- Pain in the chest – muscle tightness
- Stomach upsets
- Sweating palms
- Tremors and shakes

One of the key things to be experienced along with each of these physical symptoms to manifest themselves is all the psychological ones as well. These include suddenly feeling completely out of control, tearful, irritable, unable to control your emotions, overwhelmed by everything, and even petrified because you're convinced something bad is going to happen.

How to Win by not Fighting

Accept How You Feel

Too many times, we try to live in a state of denial. We battle to acknowledge and accept exactly what and how we are feeling. We pretend that everything's okay, instead of taking accountability and owning our emotions. So, what if you aren't strong enough to go through the day because you're too overwhelmed right now? Sometimes it's more difficult to convince ourselves that others will accept us for who and what we are right now. Instead, we believe that we need to battle everything on our own.

Be Realistic About Threats

We are very quick to immobilize ourselves with things we fear. We bring all sorts of doubts and fears directly to the forefront of our minds without actual reason or cause. Instead, we should be asking ourselves what the absolute worst thing that could happen would be. At the end of the day, re-examine your fears. Did your fears materialize? Chances are, nowhere even likely. Can you now see how important it is for you to be totally realistic about what has really happened rather than what you assume could happen?

Rely on Others

One of the biggest mistakes we make when we're faced with fear and anxiety is believing we can do it alone. The truth is that cutting yourself off from those around you only makes matters worse. Rather, share your fears and concerns with those you trust. Chances are you have a great support group of individuals who are more than willing to help you out. All you need to do is trust enough to share what's happening in your life right now.

Take Care of Yourself First

Most people suffering from chronic anxiety and fear are more concerned with those around them. You need to remember though is that, unless you've been able to take care of yourself, there's no way you can look after anyone else. It's not being selfish, it's a form of self-preservation, and being strong enough to give enough to your loved ones.

Think Positively

There are so many ways to shift your moods from anxiety and fear to positivity and hope for the future. One of the quickest ways of doing this is by changing your current environment. A couple of simple techniques to achieve this is by shifting from where you are now. Get moving. Take a walk, select some of your favorite music, dance, sing, do anything that's active. If you enjoy exercising, take yourself off to the gym for an hour or so. I can guarantee you'll begin to feel better about it. Your thoughts will clear, and you'll begin to feel more positive.

Try Mindfulness

Mindfulness is a subject all its own. I'm going to try and break it down for you as concisely as possible. It's setting your intention here and now. Living and focusing now. This moment ignores what has happened in the past. Instead of thinking about a hundred different things, you control your focus to just one thing. If you need to deal with your emotions, allow them to wash directly over you. Don't feel you need to comment on them or pass judgment. Just allow them to be. Mindfulness helps you to increase your awareness of how you are feeling about where you are right now. It shuts out all the busyness and noise of the rest of the world. You are only concerned with the here and now.

You Don't Need to Control Everything

There are simply too many moving parts when it comes to fear and anxiety. It's impossible to handle it all. You need to occasionally hand the reins over to someone else. When you begin to realize this, you can begin to get over yourself and your fear.

The entire point of this chapter has been to empower you with several techniques that aren't difficult to do, as I'm sure you'll agree. All that you need is the willingness and determination to apply them to your life. These are strategies you can use to get your emotions under control at any time throughout your life. You don't need to wait until you are so deep in a state of depression or anxiety that it becomes challenging to see your way clear.

Don't be afraid of taking control of your life right now. You've got this, even when you feel you really don't.

7 SIMPLE AND EFFECTIVE WAYS

TO BATTLE ANXIETY AND DEPRESSION WITHOUT MEDICATION

The Effective Strategies You Can Use on Your Own to Cope with Anxiety and Depression

Email RhondaJenkins786@gmail.com for your free copy

Rhonda Jenkins

Don't forget to email:
RhondaJenkins786@gmail.com
for your free copy of
The 7 Ways To Battle Anxiety

Chapter 8:

Cultivating Positive Emotion - Being Kind to Yourself

"Your life is your canvas, and you are the masterpiece. There are a million ways to be kind, amazing, fabulous, creative, bold, and interesting."

~Kerli

Techniques to Actively Take on Fears and Anxieties

There are several different techniques you can use to overcome some of the anxieties and fears we face constantly when we get into this headspace. Some of these include practicing solutions may resonate deeply with you and work for you with the time you have available.

These techniques don't only need to be used whenever you're feeling stressed out. If you can read your own body and mental stressors, you should be able to tell when an episode is about to occur. This is when to look at practicing some of these techniques.

They're not just here to help you move beyond your fears and anxieties once they're already here. You can use them to help you at any time of the day or night to prevent stress from entering your life. For many individuals, practicing some of these techniques every day helps them avoid getting into stressful situations before they occur. Let's face it, working as a preventative measure is much easier than trying to think clearly when you're in an anxious state.

Remember, the main idea is for you to be able to successfully move beyond what you're currently feeling and to return to a calmer state where you once again feel in control of your thoughts and emotions.

Remove yourself from the situation

Sometimes we're simply too close to the problem. We become so caught up in it that we can't see anything but what's currently going on. One of the best techniques to overcome these feelings is by removing yourself from a stressful situation. It becomes impossible to look for solutions to your level of concerns when it's right there in front of you. Take a couple of steps back, or away from whatever seems to be consuming your thoughts and creating anxiety in the first place. This will first give you the time to calm down, and secondly, you'll be able to look at the problem in a whole new light. One that's not directly on top of the problem.

Walking away from the current situation doesn't mean that you bury your head in the sand and pretend the problem doesn't exist at all. This means that you just allow yourself the time to regulate your thoughts and breathing before trying to tackle each problem once more. Some simple solutions to this could be as simple as running a nice hot bath and enjoying a soak, melting away the cares of the world. Easing some of the tension in your muscles without allowing your mind to wander back to the problem.

Maybe you go for a run on your favorite course. Fill your lungs with some fresh air and get some sunlight. There's nothing quite as invigorating as being able to recharge your body naturally. Something as simple as walking around and making yourself something to drink can take your mind off the problem you're experiencing. Whatever you choose to do, take a break from toxic thinking.

Back to Basics

Instead of looking at destructive coping mechanisms such as overindulging in anything from over-the-counter medication, drugs, alcohol, or other excessive behaviors, find ways to focus on simple things. It's easy to dive into a bottle as a means of trying to cope. Unfortunately, in the bright light of the following day, the problem only seems worse. Not only are you having to deal with a nasty hangover the next day and a depleted bank balance, but all your old anxieties return, many times even worse than before.

Instead of going this route, try and get back to the basics that will really help you reduce some of the stress you're feeling. As mentioned above, get some exercise, watch your eating habits, and restore your sleeping habits. You may be in such unhealthy patterns that it is going to take some time, effort, and energy to return to this kind of lifestyle. I promise it will all be worth it in the end. You'll once again begin to feel better about yourself, and this will help with some of your stress and anxiety. There's nothing more empowering than overseeing your own life once again, without leaving anything to chance.

Breathing Basics

Concentrate on the way you're breathing now. Often, this isn't something we even think about. Because it's an automatic response (and one that keeps us alive) we go through life without paying too much attention to this vital component. How does your breathing change when you're feeling stressed? Do you find yourself breathing rapidly? Is it shallow? Do you feel like you're getting lightheaded? Want to hyperventilate? Can't catch your breath? Do you feel that something heavy is on your chest, weighing you down, making it almost impossible for you to get enough air into your lungs?

Believe me, each of these responses can occur when you're experiencing fear, anxiety, and panic. The whole point of this exercise is for you to get your breathing back under control as quickly as possible. You don't want to be in any one of the above modes of breathing for an extended period.

Getting oxygen into your lungs is one of the most important things you need to do, apart from being able to regulate your breathing. If there's one thing you should do is avoid fighting the way you're feeling now. All that's going to achieve is making your breathing and emotions even more heightened than they are now.

Follow this easy step-to-step guide to get your breathing normally in no time at all:

Step 1: The quickest and easiest way to do this is by placing one hand on your stomach.

Step 2: Focus on breathing much slower, and deeper.

Step 3: Breathe in through your nose until you can feel your stomach rise. You should notice that your lungs are now filled with air.

Step 4: Try and hold this air in your lungs for the count of five.

Step 5: Slowly release the air through your mouth by pursing your lips as though you would be blowing out candles (only much slower).

Repeat this same exercise a couple of times until you can feel your breathing returning to normal and the anxiety disappears.

Cathartic Communication

There's an old expression that says that "a problem shared, is a problem halved." This really is true when we're prepared to open and discuss our feelings, emotions, thoughts, and problems with others. Admittedly, this is possibly one of the most challenging things to do. Maybe because we feel embarrassed, we're too proud, we don't want others to think that we're weak, or even that we have issues that are negatively affecting us.

This thinking is destructive and is going to not only prevent us from getting the help we need and deserve, but it's only going to make us suffer from our problem(s) for much longer than necessary. We're not always comfortable chatting with those that are closest to us about things as complex as our mental health. If this is the case, look for a support group like I did. Find a helpline closest to you. In most instances, you're able to discuss your problems with them anonymously. Those on the other side of the line have been trained to offer you sound advice, or even to just listen to you talk about your issues.

Whatever you do, don't try and bottle up your emotions. There will come a time when you explode, and chances are this will be way worse than simply opening to someone about what you're going through. Despite feeling embarrassed, you'll be surprised at how understanding and support those closest to you can be.

Heading for Happy

Visualization techniques can help you shift your mood from fear and anxiety to peace, calm, and tranquility. Think about your very own happy place, or somewhere that you feel carefree and calm. For me, it's walking along a quiet beach at sunrise. Feeling the sand squishing between my toes, waves quietly rolling in and out. I love feeling the sun on my face and the wind in my hair. Even sitting on a nearby dune and admiring the beauty around me, I can immediately put a smile on my face.

Sure, not everyone has access to a beautiful beach. Maybe for you, it's being able to listen to some of your favorite music turned all the way up or breathing some fresh icy air as you crunch your way through a winter wonderland close to your home. Maybe it's sharing hot chocolate with tiny marshmallows surrounded by your family. Whatever makes you happy, visualize yourself at that exact moment. Close your eyes and allow your mind to take you there.

This exercise may also take some practice to train your brain to go there visually, especially when you're feeling down.

Perfect People

Something we probably all suffer from is the desire to be perfect in life. We want to be the perfect spouse, the perfect parent, the perfect partner, employee/employer, child, friend, and the list could carry on. We need to face up to reality... There's no such thing as being perfect. We all make mistakes at times and, honestly, we need to make mistakes otherwise we will never learn anything.

The problem is we're so busy trying to be perfect and then holding every little mistake we make against ourselves that we become too scared to really live. We keep beating ourselves up over our mistakes. A lot of this is because we expect perfection from ourselves. We're so much quicker to forgive others, where we hold ourselves to a completely different set of standards.

Be realistic about what you expect from yourself, and think about your capacity, especially if you're battling anxiety. Remember that we all must go through the ups and downs of life. Life is what it is, it will be challenging. Your situation in life is just as unique as you are. Be aware of this and don't expect more from yourself than you're able to give. Your best is good enough.

What's the Worst?

Test your emotions and your ability to prepare for things that you may have to face and deal with by asking yourself what the absolute worst thing would be that could happen. Once you've done this, write it down in as much detail as possible. The reason for this is that you'll have something to refer to once you've gone through the experience. Almost every single time, what you've experienced will be nowhere near as bad as your imagination thought it would be.

For some reason, we always imagine the worst possible outcome. Instead of trying to be realistic about situations. Sure, it's human nature to anticipate negative outcomes. When we're depressed, or feeling anxious, our minds naturally default toward the negative rather than the positive. Question whatever you've written down and ask yourself whether what you've written is likely to happen. If it does, what's the worst you'd experience? It's highly unlikely that any of the things you've imagined will ever happen to you.

Record Your Fight Against Fear

Keeping a journal is a simple, but healthy way of working through some of the challenges and fears you may face. Journaling is a large part of CBT. It's often much easier for us to sit and write things down than to articulate the emotions we're experiencing. Remember that part of emotional stress, panic, anxiety, and depression is sometimes under pressure to be able to connect the dots properly. Having to spend some time thinking about things before you write them down can give you time for some clarity. You may not be ready to voice exactly how you're feeling to anyone else, especially not in a group setting, or to family members.

I remember feeling so embarrassed and ashamed of some of the things my husband had done. It took me a long time and a lot of work to get to the point when I realized and accepted that I wasn't the guilty party. I automatically assumed guilt, purely by being married to him.

Journaling helped me through this. Today, I can read through these journals and get a real sense of how far I've come and how much I've grown. They are a source of encouragement and inspiration to me. One of the best things about a journal is that you can keep your deepest, innermost thoughts to yourself. You may wish to share these experiences with other family members or loved ones to help them understand and appreciate your journey. Of course, this is something that's very personal and would be a decision you'd have to make for yourself.

Attack on Social Anxiety

Here we're really referring to working through panic attacks. If you've ever experienced one of these or been through a debilitating bout of depression, you'll know exactly what I mean by social anxiety. This is where you simply can't face anyone. You prefer being alone (often wallowing in self-pity). None of this is good for your mental health and well-being. This state of mind can last anything from a day or two to months.

Chances are, when you're feeling this way, not even your closest friends and loved ones can break through the barriers you've built around you. Firstly, understand that you're not alone. You're not the only person ever to have gone through this. Even though it may feel as though it's only you against the whole world right now. Statistics show that approximately 12% of all people will experience social anxiety at some stage of their lives. (Brook & Schmidt, 2008).

Some of the ways of working through social anxiety could be as simple as working through ways to relax properly, changing your current thought patterns, and facing your fears. In many of the sections above we've discussed some of the ways to relax by getting outside, speaking with others about where you are, and even focusing on changing your breathing.

A couple of other ways could be by challenging yourself to get out there and face the things that scare you the most. If you don't feel up to seeing people, start off small. Maybe you're not comfortable going out. Begin by inviting a couple of friends or loved ones over. Maybe you need to do this with baby steps first. This may be something as simple as inviting them over for tea or coffee. Work with what you can handle. If you begin to feel anxious, try and calm yourself using breathing techniques or change your scenery for a couple of minutes. Do as much as you can, this is just a starting point. Remember that the more you do, the better you'll become.

Just as you'd lay the foundation of a house and then begin building using brick and mortar—use each of these small victories as building blocks toward bigger and more challenging things. Don't push yourself beyond your actual capacity—all this will do is make matters worse and force you back into your shell. This isn't a competition, it's a way for you to work through your anxiety to get better.

War on Worry

As someone trying to work through anxiety and depression, you can appreciate the role that worry plays in making things much worse than they need be. The physical signs and symptoms of worry are bad enough. The rapid pulse, sweaty palms, increased heart rate, inability to concentrate and other symptoms make performing even the simplest tasks challenging. So, how do you manage to get over this?

Look for what's setting things off... What's the trigger? Sometimes these are obvious, while other times, you may need to really dig deep to discover exactly what's setting you off.

Some examples of common triggers could be:

- Losing a loved one unexpectedly
- Moving house
- A change in relationship status
- Changing jobs
- Drowning in debt
- Relocating to a new country or town
- Having a baby

A couple of these may seem extreme, or an obvious stressor. The point is that each of these can place you under undue pressure, resulting in worry. Coming to terms with exactly what your trigger is may take extensive thought and deep introspection. It may be worthwhile trying to journal your thoughts and emotions to identify exactly what's setting you off.

Working your way through worry includes being realistic in your thinking. Go back to asking yourself what the worst that could happen might be.

Get your breathing back under control using the breathing exercises we've already gone through.

Walk it off—take some time out in nature. This may help you by giving you a change of scenery. It's also therapeutic because you'll be getting some exercise. This will get the blood pumping, oxygen into your lungs and help exercise your muscles. You don't even need to go far. If you do something rather than remaining stuck in your own negative thoughts.

Pounding Panic

Some of the symptoms of panic attacks are rapid breathing because you find it difficult to breathe through those things, you're feeling panicked about. There are different ways to deal with this effectively. One of them we've already discussed—breathing. The main difference between this type of breathing and the other is that your focus is to slow your breathing down to the point where it's now under control. Although panic attacks are relatively harmless, they feel so much worse for the person going through this experience. If it happens to be you, chances are you're feeling out of control.

Battling to breathe is no joke. No matter how hard you try, you simply can't come to terms with the intense feelings of anxiety you're trying to deal with. Something you need to understand about panic attacks is that while they're happening, they may feel as though they're lasting forever. The truth is that they will come to an end, with no permanent damage being done, other than cutting yourself off from those around you. What you can easily do without consulting a therapist to educate yourself with as much information about this condition as possible. There are plenty of resources online.

As a caveat: Remember that not all information on the internet can be taken as being 100% accurate. Look for reputable sites, published scholarly articles, and those specializing in cognitive behavioral therapy. Look for articles that have either been published or peer-reviewed by others in the industry. Chances are you will find that many of the recommended techniques are like one another.

A worthwhile technique to try when you're battling panic attacks is learning to relax. What we're going to use for this condition is what's known as Progressive Muscle Relaxation techniques. As the name describes, it's not tense and relaxes all the muscles of the body simultaneously. Instead, it takes a staggered approach by tensing and relaxing different sets of muscles at different times.

Let me explain what I mean: this needs to be done systematically.

- Lie down comfortably on a carpet or yoga mat.
- Begin either at your head or your toes and work your way up or down. If you begin with your head, begin tensing the muscles in your face.
- Squeeze your eyes tightly closed, keeping them as tight as possible for the count of about five. Slowly begin to release this tension.
- Repeat the same proves with key muscles in your face. Move down your neck, shoulders, upper arms, torso, stomach, pelvis, upper thighs, calves, and finally your feet and toes.
- By the time you've completed this exercise, you should have felt most of the tension that was initially present simply disappear.

What's most important with panic attacks is finding something that's going to relax you, instead of winding you up further.

While we're using this technique to work through challenges you have with panic attacks, the truth is that you can use the same techniques as other CBT treatment protocols. One of the benefits of these relaxation techniques is that they don't need to take very long, but they do have long-lasting effects. Please note that these are coping strategies, they're not a magic wand that's automatically going to take all your anxiety away.

A couple of other things you may want to try to relax and get your mind off your panicked emotions include:

- Yoga
- Meditation
- Different massages
- Listening to calming music

What's most important is that these techniques and strategies make it easier for you to deal with the frustrations that come with depression and anxiety, rather than trying to eliminate these emotions.

Assaulting Agoraphobia

You may be wondering what an understandable term for agoraphobia is. Quite simply, it's the medical term for panic disorder. We already know that when you're battling with these symptoms, you're likely to go through a combination of emotions that aren't very pleasant at the time.

- Physical symptoms include:
- Erratic and disturbing thoughts
- Everything causes fear, and panic
- Nothing that's going on around you feels real
- Uncontrollable shaking
- This results in shortness of breath
- Tightening of your chest that causes you pain
- Physically, you imagine you're about to die
- Your heart may feel like it's beating out of your chest

Most of the stress and worries come from being stressed and worried that you're going to experience another panic attack. That's what Agoraphobia is. You have a panic attack because you're afraid of having a panic attack. Most of the time, you're stressed that you'll have this in front of people you know, or a crowd of people where you're likely to make a fool out of yourself. Either this or somewhere that no one can help you. This is a miserable way to try and live life.

Agoraphobia leads to avoidance. You become so afraid that you're not prepared to leave the safety of your own home, or wherever you feel most at ease, calm, and where you know that a panic attack won't happen. Of course, there's never any guarantee because panic attacks can strike at any time and without warning. The reality is that you simply don't want to give it a chance. All this additional fear prevents you from living. You're so used to wrapping yourself in cotton wool all the time that is constantly afraid prevents you from doing anything. All that staying at home and cutting yourself off from reality is going to make you feel isolated and lonely.

Having agoraphobia doesn't simply happen overnight. While it's associated with panic attacks, they really need to be bad enough, for long enough before it qualifies to be diagnosed as agoraphobia.

Practice some of the relaxation techniques we've already learned about earlier. The reason for doing this is that you can do this in the comfort of your own home without having to go somewhere that you're uncomfortable with. Another benefit of this is that you can work on relaxing whenever you want. You can use this as a preventative measure, and not just try to work through the attack itself.

You can also use your imagination to work out, which triggers set your panic attacks off initially. How this works is slowly relaxing, especially when you imagine each of the sensations and emotions that cause your attacks. The whole point of using your imagination is being able to deal with your thoughts and emotions when proper panic attacks occur.

Dealing with PTSD

Post-traumatic stress disorder or acute post-traumatic stress disorder is the result of experiencing something so traumatic that it's had a lasting effect on your mental and physical state. While we've spoken at length that CBT is about dealing with the here and now, in most instances, whatever is driving your PTSD is due to something that's happened in the past. Unfortunately, however, it's impossible for this trauma to remain in the past. In most instances, it leads to depression and anxiety.

Not all PTSD is a result of things we've been involved with ourselves- we may have witnessed something that shook us to the very core. Whatever has a negative impact on where you are now or is keeping you from living your very best life, may just be PTSD-related. You may not even remember the event because you've done so well at hiding it or blocking it in your memory that it remains hidden till it doesn't.

Some of the main causes of PTSD come from repeated abuse. This mental health disorder is almost always associated with some forms of trauma. Some of the unwanted symptoms sufferers experience are recurring nightmares where the events play out over and over in the mind or flashbacks that are so clear and vivid that you feel like you're reliving the experience all over again. It's not those sufferers want to experience each of these memories, as a matter of fact, wanting to remember is probably furthest from their minds at the time.

PTSD can result in personality and mood disorders, psychosis, anxiety, and depression. One of the worst things to happen to anyone suffering from PTSD is to be reminded of the event(s). This will act as a trigger and all these emotions are set off again. If you really want to understand what makes PTSD different, here are some of the symptoms that typical PTSD sufferers will experience:

- Avoid facing what's happened in the past
- Connecting with others and forming relationships is difficult
- Experiencing negative beliefs about self and the world around you
- Increased anxiety and awareness that's excessive
- Reliving the trauma again through vivid memories of the event
- You battle to come to terms with who you are
- You can't handle your emotions
- The associated trauma hasn't been dealt with previously. This often occurs when memories have been suppressed. The inability to remember makes these symptoms worse.
- Maybe you believe that you were somehow responsible for what happened, you blame yourself, feel guilty, or ashamed of the events. These thoughts are counterproductive.

How to Deal with PTSD

Naturally, CBT can assist with this. In most situations, the type of CBT that's used is trauma focused. Going through the process of journaling and re-journaling the experience in minute detail, and then reading each account aloud can help you understand and process your traumatic experience. What you are trying to do with CBT therapy is three-fold:

- You need to improve your self-esteem
- Learn new skills and ways to work through your symptoms
- Reduce any symptoms you may already experience

Part of CBT is learning to identify past experiences and, in many instances, forcing yourself to talk about them. Sometimes, unlocking those hidden memories is the hardest thing. You simply don't want them to be there and admitting to them is going to make them real, and reality is something we're not always ready to face.

Once you've successfully been able to identify the trauma or event, the next part is admitting that this is something that's holding you back. This may be producing fear. A fear that is deeply rooted in the past. You must bring this into the present to work through it. Whether this is with group therapy, with loved ones, or even close friends, you must learn to open up. By choosing to not do this, you're making a conscious decision to leave these experiences in the past. No part of this decision will help you move past your PTSD. You must uncover each of your fears and how bad they make you feel. In many instances, it is these fears that are not only keeping you up at night, but they're holding you back

What thought patterns are you hanging onto?

Can you identify how this event, and these thoughts are impacting your life?

Part of the journaling solution is getting all of this down on paper. It may give you the clarity that you need, as well as some ways to work through these memories. At least you'll be able to identify how this event is making you feel.

- Is there unresolved anger that needs to finally be released?
- Can you now recognize the specific fear you're trying to cope with?
- How deeply rooted is this fear?
- What is it driving you to do?
- That is, what sort of behavior are you exhibiting as your coping mechanism?
- What can you do now that will help you live with what you're experiencing?

You will find that writing out the event or trauma can help you see things from another perspective. Once you can write everything, and I mean everything down, it's time for you to look for ways to deal with each of your fears. The breathing exercises earlier in the chapter may help you to move past any anxiety you may be feeling. Try a mindfulness technique by focusing on something specific.

An example of this is focusing on a tree outside your window. Pay close attention to each of the leaves on the branches. What color are they? What shape are they? Are they blowing in a gentle breeze or about to fall off because they're crisp and brown in the autumn air? What else can you see? What do the trunk and branches look like? Are there knots in the wood? Is the bark loose and ready to fall off at any second? Are there any birds that have made the tree their home?

By focusing on something else, even for a couple of moments, can virtually 'reset' your thoughts, bringing you back into the present where you can figure out what your next step is going to be.

Remember that none of these techniques or solutions to PTSD are going to work overnight. Even with a therapist, it will take several months to work through. Be patient with yourself most of all, especially if you really want to make your life more bearable.

PTSD is something that should never be taken lightly, however, it is possible to reduce, or minimize some of your symptoms. If nothing else works, you may need to get professional help. This often requires medication to help you work through these intrusive thoughts. There's no shame in having to go this route... Remember that you need to do what is best for you.

Preventing Relapse

One of the whole points of CBT is to give you all the tools you need to avoid falling back into old patterns of negative behavior. It's easy for this to happen when you're placed under stress. Maybe you're exhausted. Each of these is a prime condition for you to fall back into your old ways again. Although this can happen quickly, it doesn't have to. Here's what you need to do:

- Identify your triggers and red flags that set off your behavior.
- Keep working through your CBT techniques and remember to reward yourself for your successes.
- Your attitude toward relapsing can influence the choices you make.

Sometimes we're so scared of having a relapse that we worry ourselves into one. This is the exact environment you're trying to avoid.

How to Work With Fear Exposure

This is something that's quite safe for you to do at home. Sufferers of fear and anxiety usually do one of two things: they either completely avoid situations that make them feel this way, or they do their best to face up to their fears and work their way through them. Whatever you decide to do is fine, however, please know that there's only so long that you can try and avoid these situations. Eventually, they will catch up to you and you'll have to face them.

Part of the solution is slowly exposing yourself to those things you fear most of all. This can be done incrementally and at your own pace. You need to be comfortable, and you are the only one that knows how much you can handle and when things become too much.

Here, are some very basic situations. Maybe some of these will resonate with you.

Eating in Public

You don't want to be seen eating in public because you feel that you're going to embarrass yourself. Facing up to this fear may begin small, but eventually, build up to where you can do this without feeling as though everyone is watching you or judging you.

There are so many ways that this disorder can negatively impact you. This can include anything from social gatherings where food is involved, business lunches, dinners, and even sitting in a work cafeteria. Choosing to avoid eating with and in front of people only adds to your anxiety. This is something that's virtually unavoidable. Avoiding it means cutting yourself off from society completely. You will reduce your social circle completely. Instead of just focusing on the food aspect, you'll begin to focus on other areas of your life as well. Eventually, shut others out of your life for good.

Treatment of this issue includes being able to understand what your triggers are. What sets off this pattern of fear? Do you only feel vulnerable in certain situations or is it all the time? Are there certain types of food that make you feel more nervous eating than others? Each of these questions needs to be asked and answered for you to come to terms with what's causing you to feel the way you do.

Public Restrooms Scare You

This fear is one of the most common fears for anyone with a social anxiety disorder. This often leads to panic attacks. You may get into such a state that you prefer to stay within the walls of your own home. After all, what could be worse than going out and having to use a restroom?

Fear exposure can slowly begin to help you get over this fear. Begin small. Maybe it's visiting friends and agreeing to use their restroom. After you feel comfortable doing this, you may choose to visit your favorite restaurant and use their facilities. Even if this is just to wash your hands and your face. Slowly build on this until you have the courage to visit a public restroom in a shopping center.

Notice how the progression and leaning into your fears are slow and steady. You're not rushing anything or forcing yourself to do something you're uncomfortable with.

Some other anxieties you may not feel comfortable with are things like:

- Being in proximity with others
- Being the center of attention
- Confrontation with others
- Fear of flying
- Public speaking
- Speaking with others on the phone
- Traveling on public transport

Common Myths About Fear Exposure

Myths surround fear of exposure, mainly because people don't understand what it is. There are three main myths that seem to have been around forever. We're going to discuss these, as well as defend each of them as we prove they're incorrect.

CBT Causes More Anxiety

Unlike avoiding those things in your life that cause anxiety, through fear exposure you can eventually face your fears and begin to lead a normal life that's comfortable for you. For those suffering from anxiety and depression, fear is a normal part of life. Without learning how to deal with fear, all that you'll continue to do is avoid it. This avoidance will lead to isolating yourself from anyone and everyone as you try and avoid having to face up to what you're uncomfortable with. Sure, fear of exposure will make you feel uncomfortable when you first start out. As time goes on, though, this will certainly become easier.

CBT Forces You Into Doing Things You Don't Want To Do

The truth is that you will only ever do those things you're comfortable with. If something makes you feel uncomfortable, you may need to leave this before trying it again at a later stage. Everything in CBT is geared toward making you feel as comfortable with your situation as possible. Nothing is forced on you. If you don't want to participate in an exercise, then this is acceptable. After all, you know yourself better than anyone else. You will never be forced to do anything you're not comfortable with. CBT only really works when you want to be part of the process.

The CBT Process is Hard Work

Absolutely. So, is nothing else in life that is going to make genuine, positive, and long-lasting changes in your life? The good news is that CBT allows you to practice repeatedly. The more you do this, the sooner you'll be able to progress from where you are now, to designing a life of peace, joy, and happiness, just like you've always wanted.

You can boost your positive emotions by making use of some of these techniques. Add them to your daily activities and watch how your negative thoughts shift.

- Journaling your blessings each day or starting a gratitude journal.
- Being more focused on using mindfulness.
- Meditating with a focus on loving-kindness
- Replace negative experiences with positive experiences. Look for the silver lining—it's there.
- Hold your head up high, keep your shoulders back and display an air of confidence.

Here's a five-step plan for you to take opposite action whenever you're feeling negative:

Step 1: Monitor your behavior for seven days.

Step 2: Identify each of the things that rob you of your energy. Get rid of each of these things. All they're doing is holding you back.

Step 3: Use brainstorming techniques to come up with pleasant activities that you can become involved with.

Step 4: Schedule of some of these activities.

Step 5: Act and be sure to participate in at least some of these activities.

Remember that this is a process. Maybe you'll get one thing done initially, that's okay, it's a start.

Chapter 9:

How You Can Stay on Track

From my personal experience, I know that when things are going great, I don't really stress about things too much, especially when I'm feeling in control of my thoughts and my life. The exact opposite when things are bad. When things are good, they're good, but I hardly know where to turn to when I'm spiralling down toward becoming an emotional wreck.

I have no clue as to why falling back into negative habits can be so easy or comfortable. Some of these negative thought patterns that seem to return unapologetically are thought distortions where we believe everything we think about. Because thoughts cross our minds, they must, of course, be true. It makes sense why we need to guard our thoughts so carefully, especially when they focus on:

- Guilt and shame
- Not understanding where stress comes from
- Self-criticism
- Blaming ourselves for everything in the past, present, and future

Watch Your Thinking

Remember that what we think not only determines how we view ourselves but can have a devastating effect on those around us, our family, friends, relationships with work colleagues and associates. Our thinking can make us feel less than important, resulting in low self-esteem. Our physical and mental health is likely to suffer because of this type of thinking.

So, there are right and wrong ways of going about this. Let's look at some of the things you should really try and keep away from:

- Remember we briefly mentioned some of the eating disorders right at the beginning of this book. No matter whether you binge-eat, or pretend to eat, only to go down the anorexia or bulimia rabbit hole. None of these things are positive. In fact, they can have a devastating effect on your life. If you know that you have a problem when it comes to eating, please add this to your list of things to work through using CBT techniques.

- Any form of abuse—drugs, alcohol, prescription drugs, over-the-counter medication, or any other form of abuse simply doesn't work. This acts as a very short-term solution to taking your "pain" away. However, you're likely to beat yourself up even more for being too weak to stick with decisions you may have already made regarding your recovery.

There are four steps that can help you move past self-sabotage and negative thinking:

Recognize Negative Thinking for What it is

These are all those emotions that we've been trying to get rid of throughout this book so far. Things like guilt, shame, fear, anxiety, depression, hopelessness. Whenever we feel unwanted, unloved, or unworthy of anything good, these are all negative thoughts that we need to stop dead in their tracks.

The moment you can call each of these thoughts out for exactly what they are—negative and destructive, you can begin to question their validity. You don't need to believe them because you can see they're not true. Remember that thoughts are just that. When you practice mindfulness, you can allow each negative thought to simply pass over you without paying too much attention. The last thing you want to do is to feed your negative thinking. If your thinking is not building you up, they're breaking you down and aren't worth it.

Past Regrets

It's quite normal for us to have things in the past that we regret. It's all part of life. Remember that there's no such thing as having a perfect life or being a perfect person. This is a pipe dream. There's a massive difference between living a life filled with regrets over everything. This will paralyze you now and make it extremely difficult to make any decision. I'm sure you'll agree that it doesn't matter who you are or where you are on your journey through life, and you will always need to make choices and decisions. Being paralyzed and unable to do this will lead to further anxiety and stress. All the things you're trying to avoid.

I love this quote by the author and psychotherapist, Amy Morin (n.d.). It just proves that we need to recognize mistakes and failures as opportunities for us to grow.

"Sticking to good habits can be hard work, and mistakes are part of the process. Don't declare failure simply because you messed up or because you're having trouble reaching your goals. Instead, use your mistakes as opportunities to grow stronger and become better."

Are You Worrying Unnecessarily?

When you open your mind to worrying, it's like opening the flood gates to allow pure negativity into your head. Let's face it, there are so many things that you can worry about—the economy, the weather, politics, your children, your health, your work, your family, your finances, and the list can go on forever. Chances are though that most of what we're worried about will never happen. Our imaginations can run wild with us if we choose to let them. We live in the fantasy world of "what if this happens," or "what would I do if this went wrong?" Living your life like this will only bring additional stress into your life.

Listening to Your Inner Critic

This is that little voice often screams so loudly in your head that it manages to drown out whatever positive thoughts you have going on. All that this voice does is criticize everything you do. It's that voice that constantly beats us up over every little action or decision we make. This becomes a habit, one that only results in a lack of self-esteem, depression, and even thoughts of taking your own life. You believe that the world and everyone in it would be better off without you.

You can move past each of these things by monitoring yourself. Working through each challenging experience will help you heal and become a better person. Many of these points have already been discussed. This serves as a reminder because each of them is so vitally important to understand and put into practice.

Own Your Feelings

Identify and name each of the feelings you're experiencing. If you're angry, don't be afraid to say that you're feeling angry. What is important, though, is being able to say what's making you angry. Remember that your feelings and emotions are yours, and yours alone. Making the statement that someone makes you feel in some way is incorrect. We need to acknowledge that we are the only ones in control of our emotions. We need to own the way we're feeling, rather than blaming our emotions on someone else.

Talk to Someone

Don't feel embarrassed about talking about what you're going through with someone you trust. If you are ashamed about your situation, then you may want to chat with a counselor or a therapist or in an anonymous group setting. And yes, sometimes offloading to a stranger can be therapeutic.

Many individuals attending group therapy sessions have and are in similar situations. They're less likely to judge you. Maybe, like me, you have an excellent support structure of friends and family who just want what's best for you. They're more than happy to just listen to you. They'll offer advice, only if you want it. These are exactly the type of individuals you want and need in your corner.

Surround Yourself with Positive People

Whatever you do, avoid those people that are going to make your current situation worse. If you surround yourself with people who are going to judge you or make you feel responsible for what you're experiencing now, it's time to cut ties with them. When you're already feeling like a failure, you need someone who's going to encourage you and help you find solutions, rather than even more problems.

Look for Lessons

Instead of looking at a bad situation as completely negative, change the narrative and think about what you can learn from the experience instead. No matter what you're going through, or have been through in your life, there are always lessons to be learned. Even if it's coming to terms with the fact that you're a survivor.

Prioritize Yourself

Make yourself a priority. If you're not going to care about yourself, then how can you expect anyone else to care for you? Even when you don't feel like it, which, let's face it, happens often when you're feeling anxious or depressed. These are the times when you need to force yourself to try. You'll feel better about it, I promise.

Find the Positives

Sure, we've also spoken quite a bit about changing the way you think and looking for positive rather than negative. What's more important in CBT is being able to recognize and acknowledge what's happening right now. Are your thoughts accurate? Can you support them with actual evidence, or is your thinking flawed? Facing up to reality is the basis of all CBT.

Call an End and Just Take Action

Decide to cut off thoughts or behaviors that are destructive. You can make this decision, you know. Even though you may feel helpless, you have the power to put an end to negative beliefs and thinking. If there's something you're doing that's destructive, you are the only one who can change your thoughts. You are the one that can decide to act rather than waiting and watching from the sidelines.

Limit Your Time with Toxic People

These are those who love nothing more than to see you fail, be miserable, and wallow in self-pity. In fact, they are the same ones who will blame you for being in your current situation. Instead of support, they're happy to offer advice that's destructive rather than valid. The world is full of toxic individuals who are normally so self-absorbed that they seldom have time for anyone else. If you're already feeling nervous, anxious, sad, or depressed, these are the last people you need to be around.

Observe From the Outside and Stay Grounded

Often, we get caught up in our thoughts and emotions because we're so close to them. Sometimes, we need to look at things from another perspective. It helps to take a couple of steps back and re-examine your current experiences as though you were an outsider looking in. Instead of getting carried away by negative thinking, stay focused on what is happening right here and right now. It's important that you remain grounded in this moment rather than in the past or in the future. Remember that the past is exactly that. It's over and there's little you can do to change it. The future is in the distance. Although we can plan for it, there's little we can do to control it. The only thing we really have is the present. This time, this very moment is all we should be concerned about.

Everyone Heals Differently

Be patient with yourself, especially when things seem to be taking much longer than you would like. Remember that everyone heals differently. There's no single timetable that starts and ends at a specific time. What may take someone a couple of weeks, could take another person-years to reach the same point in their healing process. Don't compare yourself and where you are on your journey. This is individual therapy, with individual and unique treatments and outcomes. Your healing will occur naturally, as, and when it's supposed to.

You Are Not Your Bad Situation

It was very easy for me to blame myself for the actions of my husband. I took on all the guilt, shame, and embarrassment. Sure, I had not asked to be placed in the situation my children and I found ourselves in. Although I was carrying all this emotional baggage around with me, I needed to learn that what I was going through did not define me as an individual. The shame and guilt were my husband's rather than ours. CBT was the only form of therapy that helped me recognize this. It was exactly what I needed to face life again with my head held high.

Even when life gets tough and you feel like you simply can't go on anymore, and there will be days when you do feel like this, remember that you are much tougher than you give yourself credit for. You can do this. There's always hope for a brighter future and a better life. Tough times don't last forever.

Chapter 10:

Conclusion

"Believe in yourself and all that you are. Know that there is something inside you that is greater than any obstacle."

~ Christian D. Larson

Each of the previous chapters has focused on different areas of CBT and exactly how this therapy can be used to help us overcome some of the toughest challenges we will ever face in our lives. In most instances, we aren't the cause of our stress, anxiety, debilitating depression, and any other mental health disorder. What we are responsible for, though, is what we do about it.

I'm not going to sugar-coat anything; no mental illness is pleasant. Chances are you will be dealing with it for the rest of your life. This is where being able to self-regulate thanks to CBT interventions can be so important. It's the lifeline that most of us need. As mentioned right at the beginning of this book, the purpose of each chapter is for it to be used as a reference section.

Please know that experiencing panic attacks, depression, anxiety, feeling aggressive toward those you love suddenly, feeling like you want to be left alone, or relying on addictions to make you feel better are all connected. They all form part of the underlying mental disorders.

No matter what anyone has to say about you or to you, mental illness is something that's very real. However, the thoughts and emotions you experience because of this doesn't define who you are as a person. The only one who has control over how you feel about yourself is you. You determine who you are now and who you want to be in the future. It's up to you to decide whether you're prepared to listen to the negativity of the world or the inner critic in your head. You can redefine yourself by changing your beliefs.

Being able to practice CBT is not about sweeping your problems under the rug and pretending that there is nothing wrong with your life. It's being able to look at your thoughts, emotions, and behaviors realistically, identifying those areas that need to be changed, and then trying to change these things.

I want you to know that it is possible to move past each negative thought pattern. You can replace them with something more positive, something better. You now have all the tools you need to be able to self-regulate using CBT techniques. Remember that it's going to take practice until some of these become like second nature to you. While you are working on some of the different techniques and ways to deal with depression and anxiety, know that it's going to take time. Don't become frustrated when things don't go your way, or you happen to relapse. Hey, it's all part of the process. It's all part of the healing that needs to occur. Being patient with yourself is one of the toughest calls, yet it can also be the most rewarding form of treatment there.

What really needs to be mentioned as part of becoming whole again is that you should only take on as much as you can handle mentally and emotionally. In CBT, it's recommended that you work through just one issue at a time. This makes perfect sense. You don't want to try and tackle multiple issues all at the same time. Working through one stressor in your life can help you build small successes along the way. This is something that you need to help you build your self-esteem after all.

Now that you know what to do, it's time for you to get out there and design the life that you really want. Even if you are doing this at a snail's pace. At least you are doing something about it, rather than wallowing in self-pity or trying to lay the blame for what you're experiencing at someone else's door. Sure, they may be guilty of putting you into the position you now find yourself in. However, it doesn't help to try to close the barn door once the horse has bolted. All you can do is search for the horse to bring it back safely. This is the same attitude you need to have when dealing with anxiety, depression, and all other mental health-related illnesses.

All you need to do is to decide to start. Remember to focus on one small thing at a time. Take smaller steps until you become more confident. Even then, the secret to CBT is working on one key area at a time. There's no competition to see who's going to get over how they are feeling all at once. The goal is to get better. To help you move beyond your anxiety and depression. Be realistic in your expectations. In many instances, CBT therapy is something that should be ongoing. We already know that there's very little you can do to control where your thoughts go. What you do have control over, however, is how you act or react to each of those thoughts.

- What are your goals, can you clearly identify what you see for yourself in the future?
- Do you know how you plan to get there?
- What is the very first step you need to take?
- Is it possible for you to take that step without feeling overwhelmed or out of your depth?

If this is how you're feeling, then the chances are that your goals are way too big. You need to break them down further.

As you begin to work on the way you behave, how you feel, and how you think, you will begin to see positive changes taking place in your life. This is all that I wish for you. To have a bright future where you're filled with confidence and can once again step out into the sunlight without carrying negative baggage around with you.

As an author, I value your input as the reader and customer. Please leave a review in the section provided. Here's wishing you all the joy, peace, and happiness you deserve and so much more.

References

Ackerman, C. E. (2018, February 12). CBT's cognitive restructuring (CR) for tackling cognitive distortions. PositivePsychology.com. https://positivepsychology.com/cbt-cognitive-restructuring-cognitive-distortions/

Amy Morin Quotes. (n.d.). Amy Morin Quotes | Sticking to good habits. BrainyQuote. https://www.brainyquote.com/quotes/amy_morin_944000?src=t_sticking/

Ankrom, S. (2020, July 8). The difference between fear and anxiety. Verywell Mind; Verywellmind. https://www.verywellmind.com/fear-and-anxiety-differences-and-similarities-2584399

Anxiety Canada. (n.d.). Self Help - Cognitive-Behavioural Therapy (CBT). Anxiety Canada. https://www.anxietycanada.com/articles/self-help-cognitive-behavioural-therapy-cbt/

Arocho, J. (2015, November 23). How CBT uses goal setting. Manhattan Center for Cognitive Behavioral Therapy. https://www.manhattancbt.com/archives/544/cbt-uses-goal-setting/

Bence, S. (2021, February 15). Anxiety symptoms. Verywell Health. https://www.verywellhealth.com/anxiety-symptoms-5086955

Brook, C. A., & Schmidt, L. (2008). Social anxiety disorder: A review of environmental risk factors. Neuropsychiatric Disease and Treatment, 4(1), 123. https://doi.org/10.2147/ndt.s1799

Cherney, K. (2020, August 25). Effects of anxiety on the body. Healthline. https://www.healthline.com/health/anxiety/effects-on-body

Cherry, K. (2020). Cognitive behavioral therapy. Verywell Mind; Verywellmind. https://www.verywellmind.com/what-is-cognitive-behavior-therapy-2795747

Christian D. Larson Quote. (n.d.). Christian D. Larson Quote | PCOS Living. Treatments to Manage PCOS Symptoms | PCOS Living. Retrieved October 6, 2021, from https://www.pcosliving.com

Cognitive Behavioral Therapy Los Angeles. (n.d.-a). Identifying automatic thoughts in CBT. Cognitive Behavioral Therapy Los Angeles. https://cogbtherapy.com/cbt-and-automatic-thoughts

Cognitive Behavioral Therapy Los Angeles. (n.d.-b). The CBT model of emotions. Cognitive Behavioral Therapy Los Angeles. https://www.cogbtherapy.com/cbt-model-of-emotions/

cortez13. (n.d.). Staircase in mist. In Pixabay. https://pixabay.com/photos/mountains-hiking-trail-the-fog-1143626/

Cuncic, A. (2019, September 10). What to do if you fear eating in public. Verywell Mind. https://www.verywellmind.com/why-am-i-afraid-to-eat-in-front-of-people-3024319

Cuncic, A. (2020a, March 20). Social anxiety activities to get better. Verywell Mind. https://www.verywellmind.com/social-anxiety-disorder-tips-3024209

Cuncic, A. (2020b, September 19). 7 Types of social fears and the best way to overcome them. Verywell Mind. https://www.verywellmind.com/practice-social-anxiety-disorder-exposure-therapy-3024845

Cuncic, A. (2021, September 1). Negative thoughts: How to stop them. Verywell Mind. https://www.verywellmind.com/how-to-change-negative-thinking-3024843

Elmer, J. (2021, July 1). 5 Ways to stop spiraling negative thoughts from taking control. Healthhline.com. https://www.healthhline.com/health/mental-health/stop-automatic-negative-thoughts

Fritscher, L. (2020, April 28). What is fear? Verywell Mind; Verywellmind. https://www.verywellmind.com/the-psychology-of-fear-2671696

Good Therapy. (2015). Exposure therapy. Www.goodtherapy.org. https://www.goodtherapy.org/learn-about-therapy/types/exposure-therapy

Hartney, E. (2020, November 30). 10 Cognitive distortions that can lead to addiction relapse. Verywell Mind. https://www.verywellmind.com/ten-cognitive-distortions-identified-in-cbt-22412

Herndon, J. (2021, June 10). What to know about exposure therapy for anxiety. Healthline. https://www.healthline.com/health/anxiety/exposure-therapy-for-anxiety

Hirschlag, A. (2020, December 19). Do you live with anxiety? Here are 11 ways to cope. Healthline; Healthline Media. https://www.healthline.com/health/mental-health/how-to-cope-with-anxiety

International Bipolar Foundation. (n.d.). Putting your thoughts on trial: How to use CBT thought records. International Bipolar Foundation. https://ibpf.org/putting-your-thoughts-on-trial-how-to-use-cbt-thought-records/

Julson, E. (2021, September 15). Signs and symptoms of anxiety disorders. Healthline. https://www.healthline.com/health/anxiety-disorder-symptoms

Keiffenheim, E. (2020, May 24). To transform your life, start changing your thoughts. Change Your Mind Change Your Life. https://medium.com/change-your-mind/to-transform-your-life-start-changing-your-thoughts-fc0efc423b69

Kerli Quotes. (n.d.). Kerli Quotes | Be kind. BrainyQuote. https://www.brainyquote.com/quotes/kerli_936062?src=t_be_kind/

Lebow, H. I. (2021, July 22). What causes irrational thoughts and can you manage them? Psych Central. https://psychcentral.com/lib/stop-irrational-thoughts

Mark Tyrrell's Therapy Skills. (2016, March 7). 3 Instantly Calming CBT Techniques for Anxiety. Mark Tyrrell's Therapy Skills. https://www.unk.com/blog/3-instantly-calming-cbt-techniques-for-anxiety/

Mcleod, S. (2019). Cognitive behavioral therapy. Simplypsychology.org. https://www.simplypsychology.org/cognitive-therapy.html

NHS Health Scotland. (2021, April 14). Ten ways to fight your fears. Www.nhsinform.scot. https://www.nhsinform.scot/healthy-living/mental-wellbeing/fears-and-phobias/ten-ways-to-fight-your-fears

NHS UK. (2021, February 8). Cognitive behavioural therapy (CBT). Nhs.uk. https://www.nhs.uk/mental-health/talking-therapies-medicine-treatments/talking-therapies-and-counselling/cognitive-behavioural-therapy-cbt/

O'Brien, M. (2018, August 20). 4 Keys to overcoming negative thinking for good - Melli O'Brien. Mrs. Mindfulness. https://mrsmindfulness.com/the-four-keys-to-overcoming-negative-thinkingfor-good/

O'Keefe Osborn, C. (2019, February 27). Common and unique fears explained. Healthline. https://www.healthline.com/health/list-of-phobias

Owen, D., Shiloff, N., Tanner, L., & Tompkins, M. A. (2020, September 19). Facing your fears: Dispelling the myths of exposure therapy | Psychology Today. Www.psychologytoday.com. https://www.psychologytoday.com/us/blog/anxious-minds/202009/facing-your-fears-dispelling-the-myths-exposure-therapy

Psychology Tools. (n.d.-a). Post-Traumatic stress disorder (PTSD). Psychology Tools. https://www.psychologytools.com/professional/problems/post-traumatic-stress-disorder-ptsd/

Psychology Tools. (n.d.-b). Thoughts in CBT. Psychology Tools. https://www.psychologytools.com/self-help/thoughts-in-cbt/

Raypole, C. (2019, June 26). Cognitive behavioral therapy: How CBT works. Healthline. https://www.healthline.com/health/cognitive-behavioral-therapy

Reinecke, A., Thilo, K. V., Croft, A., & Harmer, C. J. (2018). Early effects of exposure-based cognitive behaviour therapy on the neural correlates of anxiety. Translational Psychiatry, 8(1). https://doi.org/10.1038/s41398-018-0277-5

Schwantes, M. (2018, April 3). 8 Successful mental habits to defeat fear, worry, and anxiety. Inc.com. https://www.inc.com/marcel-schwantes/8-mental-hacks-that-will-keep-you-strong-under-control-during-tough-times.html

Selva, J. (2017, April 3). What is cognitive behavioral therapy (CBT)? A psychologist explains. PositivePsychology.com. https://positivepsychology.com/what-is-cbt-definition-meaning/

Soeiro, L. (2018, October 25). Instant CBT: The simplest way to challenge negative thoughts. Psychology Today. https://www.psychologytoday.com/za/blog/i-hear-you/201810/instant-cbt-the-simplest-way-challenge-negative-thoughts

Stanborough, R. J. (2020, February 4). How to change negative thinking with cognitive restructuring. Healthline. https://www.healthline.com/health/cognitive-restructuring

Star, K. (2020a, September 17). How to cope with Agoraphobia. Verywell Mind. https://www.verywellmind.com/homebound-with-agoraphobia-2583911

Star, K. (2020b, September 17). How to overcome your fear of panic attacks. Verywell Mind; Verywellmind. https://www.verywellmind.com/tips-for-overcoming-a-fear-of-panic-attacks-2584109

Steimle, J. (2016, January 4). 14 Ways to conquer fear. Forbes. https://www.forbes.com/sites/joshsteimle/2016/01/04/14-ways-to-conquer-fear/?sh=4467d8e51c48

Sutton, J. (2020, June 19). Socratic questioning in psychology: Examples and techniques. PositivePsychology.com. https://positivepsychology.com/socratic-questioning/

Thich Nhat Hanh Quotes. (n.d.). Thich Nhat Hanh Quotes | Fear keeps us focused. BrainyQuote. https://www.brainyquote.com/quotes/thich_nhat_hanh_531574/

Treehouse Recovery. (n.d.). Cognitive Behavioral Therapy -- Relapse Prevention (CBT-RP). Treehouse Recovery. https://treehouserecovery.com/evidence-based/cognitive-behavioral-therapy-relapse-prevention-cbt-rp/

Whalley, M. (2019, January 10). Delivering more effective exposure therapy in CBT | Psychology Tools. Psychology Tools. https://www.psychologytools.com/articles/delivering-more-effective-exposure-therapy-in-cbt/

Whalley, M., & Kaur, H. (n.d.). What is cognitive behavioral therapy (CBT)? Psychology Tools. https://www.psychologytools.com/self-help/what-is-cbt/

Yetman, D. (2021, June 21). Exposure therapy. Healthline. https://www.healthline.com/health/exposure-therapy

Printed in Great Britain
by Amazon

27142417R00077